Jan-Hendrik Kuntze

The Abolishment of the Right to Privacy?

Jan-Hendrik Kuntze

The Abolishment of the Right to Privacy?

The USA, Mass Surveillance and the Spiral Model

Tectum Verlag

Jan-Hendrik Kuntze

The Abolishment of the Right to Privacy? The USA, Mass Surveillance and the Spiral Model

ISBN: 978-3-8288-4034-8
eISBN: 978-3-8288-6953-0

Printed in Germany

Besuchen Sie uns im Internet
www.tectum-verlag.de

Bibliografische Informationen der Deutschen Nationalbibliothek
Die Deutsche Nationalbibliothek verzeichnet diese Publikation in der Deutschen Nationalbibliografie; detaillierte bibliografische Angaben sind im Internet über http://dnb.ddb.de abrufbar.

List of Abbreviations

ACLU	American Civil Liberties Union
AFSA	Armed Forces Security Agency
AFSS	Air Force Security Service
AI	Amnesty International
ASA	Army Security Agency
CAHDATA	Council of Europe's Ad Hoc Committee on Data Protection
CALEA	Communication Assistance for Law Enforcement Act of 1994
CCC	Chaos Computer Club
CHR	Council of Europe's Commissioner of Human Rights
CIA	Central Intelligence Agency
CoE	Council of Europe
COINTELPRO	Counter Intelligence Program
COMINT	Communications Intelligence
DARPA	Defense Advanced Research Project Agency
EDPS	European Data Protection Supervisor
EFF	Electronic Frontier Foundation
EP	European Parliament
EPIC	Electronic Privacy Information Center
EU	European Union
FAA	Foreign Intelligence Surveillance Amendments Act of 2008
FBI	Federal Bureau of Investigations
FISA	Foreign Intelligence Surveillance Act of 1978
FISC	Foreign Intelligence Surveillance Court
FTC	Federal Trade Commission
GPEN	Global Privacy Enforcement Network
HRC	United Nations Human Rights Council
IAO	Information Awareness Office
ICC	International Criminal Court
ICCPR	International Covenant on Civil and Political Rights

ICESCR	International Covenant on Economic, Social and Cultural Rights
IDC	Information Dominance Center
IO	International Organization
(I)NGO	(International) Non-Governmental Organization
ISP	Internet Service Provider
LIBE	European Parliament's Committee on Civil Liberties, Justice and Home Affairs
NSA	National Security Agency
NSG	Naval Security Group
NSL	National Security Letter
OECD	Organization for Economic Co-Operation and Development
OPR	Office of Professional Responsibility
PAA	Protect America Act of 2007
PCLOB	Privacy and Civil Liberties Oversight Board
PPD	Presidential Policy Directive
PSP	President's Surveillance Program
SRP	United Nation's Special Rapporteur on Privacy
SSA	Signal Security Agency
SIGINT	Signals Intelligence
TIA	Total Information Awareness Program
TSP	Terrorist Surveillance Program
TTIP	Transatlantic Trade and Investment Partnership
UDHR	Universal Declaration of Human Rights
UN	United Nations

Table of Contents

1. Introduction

More than four years ago, on June 5, 2013, the *Guardian* published the first article revealing the surveillance of communications and Internet usage of both American citizens and a huge number of people around the world – conducted by the USA and their allies. The accusations were based on documents published by whistleblower and National Security Agency (NSA) intelligence analyst Edward Snowden (Greenwald 2013 a). In the following months, further newspaper articles revealed more details of what would become known as the NSA affair. The disclosures turned out to be a violation of a human rights norm: the right to privacy that is stated in Article 12 of the Universal Declaration of Human Rights (UDHR).

This violation of the norm will be scrutinized in this book. First of all, it will be a matter of interest how this norm violating behavior has developed. Second, and according to the spiral model – a theory that aims to explain the adoption of human rights norms by nation states – a human rights advocacy network should be in place to punish the norm violation and to push the norm violator back to a stage of rule-consistent behavior. Whether this advocacy network was activated and whether the main violator, the United States of America (USA), have been influenced by this advocacy process will be another sphere of interest. Thereby, this paper aims to contribute to the existing research literature by developing a first draft of a model that is capable of explaining both the adoption and the denial of a norm by a nation state.

The compliance of states with international norms has attracted the attention especially of political scientists for decades. Since the decolonization and the emergence of the European Union (EU), constructivism has established itself into the research field of international relations. Specifically with regard to the acceptance of human rights norms, constructivist scholars in the 1990 s aimed to discover how norms emerge in the international arena and how they achieve political influence at the international and domestic level. The most prominent approaches to theorizing about the emergence of human rights norms were made by Martha Finnemore and Kathryn Sikkink (1998), who invented the *life cycle* of norms, and by Thomas Risse et al. (1999), who crafted the *spiral model*. The life cycle is mainly based on the development of normative argumentation to explain the international emergence of a norm and consists of three steps. First, the norm emerges by being advocated by so-called *norm entrepreneurs*; second, due to a *tipping point* (war, crisis etc.) the norm *cascades*, which means that it resonates with a large audience and the argumentation of norm entrepreneurs convinces more and more people; finally, the norm is internalized and henceforth taken as a given. This means that the norm will never be questioned anymore. Nevertheless, this does not mean that the life cycle is inevitable: a norm does not necessarily have to complete the life cycle (Finnemore & Sikkink 1998: 895ff.). However, Antje Wiener (2014) developed a *theory of contestation* that was one of the first attempts to theorize the objection to predominating norms.

The spiral model, on the other hand, tries to explain the domestic adoption of an international norm and contextualizes the domestic acknowledgement. The spiral model explains the variation of norm adoption and the lack of progress. However, it does not explain how a norm emerges in more general terms. The spiral model already presupposes the existence of a norm advocacy network that pressures a state to comply with a norm. Meaning the norm has already cascaded at the international level (Risse et al. 1999: 1ff.).

Apart from the differences between these two models, both have in common that they are mainly based on rhetorical arrangements (normative argumentation) in social communities to explain the institutionalization of a norm. They are the precondition for the establishment of human rights norms. As Heller et al. (2012: 280 f.) emphasizes, the public justification of state actions are not trivial. Instead, discursive legitimization of state actions is necessary to secure and enlarge the room to maneuver in the long run. In other words, a behavior that violates a norm does not mean that the particular norm is not existent anymore. To obtain a far-reaching acceptance of the behavior of a state in the public as well as in the international arena, the behavior has to be justified with normative arguments that are shared by most international and domestic actors.

However, in recent time, both the life cycle and the spiral model have been criticized for having limitations. Both models assume that a norm, after being internalized, will never be questioned. Hence, they do not provide tools to explain the regression of norms. Furthermore, it has been criticized that the work of constructivism had mainly concentrated on the distribution of *good norms* and had neglected *bad norms* and *negative ideas* which can also drive the actions of states (Liese 2009: 19; McKeown 2009: 6ff.; Heller et al. 2012: 281).

Thus, scholars started to remove the "teleological flavor" (McKeown 2009: 7) from the norm literature. This research focus was driven by the counterterrorism policy of many Western states because scholars observed a regression of human rights norms in discourse and state actions due to the war on terror. Whereas Liese (2009) worked out the details of argumentative norm contestation, Heller et al. (2012) have shown that the life cycle of norms can also be employed to explain the rise of the security norm, which has interfered with human rights norms since 9/11 and serves as a justification for counterterrorism policy. Besides this, the first to invent a theory of norm regress was McKeown (2009). He explored the regression of the prohibition of torture using a reverse life cycle. In the first step, norm revisionists challenge an internalized norm. This is not necessarily to be done by discursive measures only but with the implementation of a practice violating the existing norm. This "secretive change in practice" (11) is accompanied by a legitimating discourse and "will leave the prescriptive status of the norm intact" (11). However, this norm challenge can provoke a *reverse cascade* in which the counter norm resonates, and the arguments in favor of a norm challenge proliferate. According to McKeown (2009), the formerly internalized norm is weakened by the sole action of public contestation, even if defenders of the norm are successful in defending the norm against revisionists arguments in the first place. Nonetheless, the resonance of the contesting norm will grow over time. While the first stage of the reverse cascade happens in domestic discourse, at the same time the standing of the norm is weakened at the international level. Other actors anticipate the weakness of the norm and are influenced by the discursive arguments of the norm revisionists. In the very end, this can lead to the last step of norm regress, the expiration of the norm (McKeown 2009: 11 f.).

However, this concept is not exempt from criticism either. As Heller et al. (2012) explains, the norm death series exhibit the weakness of not being able to explain that "under 'usual' contestation processes norms get only temporarily off balance and may ultimately lead to the reaffirmation of the established norm. A number of global reactions to US counterterrorism policy [...] might have limited the momentum of the 'bad' norm cascade" (283). Because this model fails to represent the dynamics of discourse in societies, I argue that further attempts have to be made to theorize about the process of norm regress and how it interacts with the process of norm diffusion. This book aims to make a contribution to this field.

On the following pages, the regression of the privacy norm is ascertained. This is done with the goal of testing the applicability of the spiral model to the development of norm regression. The main question to be explored is if the spiral model can be reversed similar to the life cycle to explain the regression of a human rights norm.

Because privacy is a weak and less precise norm, it is beyond the scope of this paper to analyze the contemporary condition of the privacy norm on the international level and in every part of the world. Hence, and because the spiral model aims to explain the domestic behavior of a single state and not the process of the creation of a norm as such, the norm regress should be exemplified in a case study on the USA. As the NSA affair has exhibited, communications and informational privacy is not valued by the USA domestically and internationally. Hence, this paper concentrates on the regression of communications and informational privacy in the USA. In addition, the USA is a prime example because their surveillance activities are well explored.

As already mentioned by Heller et al. (2012: 278 f.), surveillance measures have increased specifically in the US and Europe based on the counter norm that has been challenging human rights norms for more than a decade: security. Nevertheless, in the case of the USA, one must realize that the contestation of the privacy norm did not begin with the 9/11 terror attacks in New York and Washington, D.C., but with the domestic legal establishment of the norm in the 1930s. Taking this into account, this paper explores the development of surveillance measures justified by security concerns and their influence on the norm of privacy in the USA in the long run. At the end of this case study, a *comprehensive spiral model* is drafted that connects the processes of norm diffusion and norm regression.

Albeit the spiral model aims to explain domestic behavior, the NSA affair also has an international dimension. The evolution of global communications and informational mass surveillance is also analyzed briefly in this paper, and the capability of the spiral model to explain this development is tested as well, although this is not the main focus of this book.

As mentioned before, a connection has to be made between the processes of norm regression and norm diffusion. Therefore, not only the degradation of the norm privacy is explored in this paper but also the advocacy process that follows the discovered norm violation conducted by the USA in 2013. Because of that, the second research question is whether an advocacy process for the privacy norm followed the norm violation of the USA and if this advocacy process was able to pressure the USA to rule-consistent behavior. In other words, is the norm privacy in the process of dying, like it is occasionally portrayed in the public (Kittlitz 2010), or not? The original spiral model is employed to highlight this issue. By doing this, the paper provides one of the first theoretical approaches to characterize the responses to the Snowden revelations.

This paper proceeds as follows to gain answers on both research questions. In the second chapter the spiral model is exposed. Chapter three describes the diffusion of the norm privacy, how it became an international norm and how this norm can be defined. Subsequently, chapter four details the case study on the USA; it explores the contestation of communications and informational privacy domestically (and, in part, internationally). The chapter results in the development of a first draft of a comprehensive spiral model that aims to explain both the rise and regress of human rights norms. In the following, chapters five and six analyze the reactions of selected privacy norm entrepreneurs to the Snowden revelations as well as the response of the USA with the aid of the spiral model. Last but not least, a conclusion is drawn in chapter seven.

2. The Spiral Model

On the occasion of the fiftieth anniversary of the UDHR, scholars Thomas Risse, Stephen Ropp, and Kathryn Sikkink published *The Power of Human Rights* (1999) whose centerpiece was the invention of the spiral model. At that time, the upcoming and rising interests of scholars in norm distribution helped to shape the book. The book aimed to find out whether the principles stated in the UDHR effectively changed the behavior of states, what were the causes and determinants of this change and why these norms were implemented to a different degree by different countries. To explain these variations, they proposed the spiral model. Due to some criticism, the scholars launched a revised edition of the book named *The Persistent Power of Human Rights* (2013), first published in 2011. The following statements are based on the updated version (Risse et al. 2013: 5–25).

The model relies on the basic assumption that states act like individuals when it comes to norm diffusion. It presupposes that there is a group's (or society's) collective understanding of an accepted behavior (norms and values) and that this socializes the members of this society. By this process of socialization, the group influences the member's interests, identity and behavior so that it is in line with the values accepted by society. Hence, if a state wants to belong to the international society of states, it will have to agree to the norms of this society and have to adopt a rule-consistent behavior through the change of domestic practices. According to the spiral model, this process of socialization can be compartmentalized into five single steps.

The first step is called *repression* and activation of the network. Through national non-governmental organizations (NGOs) or opposition groups, information about human rights violations conducted by a repressing state are sent to a transnational network (which are the guards of the international human rights regime) consisting of international organizations (IOs), international non-governmental organizations (INGOs) and liberal (rule-consisting) states.[1] These norm-promoting agents initiate an advocacy process in which the repressive regime is confronted with this information, and a lobbying process is set up to blame the repressive state. Hence, the repressing state is pressured *from above* and *from below,* albeit the domestic opposition remains relatively weak to this point because of possible repression by the norm violating state.

Nevertheless, this evokes, second, a *How dare you!* reaction of the repressive state showing an ongoing refusal to recognize the international human rights norms. This phase is called *denial.* The transnational network is strengthened by this denial of international norms and will increase its effort to prove the violating state wrong. Additionally, in most cases this step gives the opportunity to begin a conversation between the repressing state and the international society.

As a third step, in order to get rid of the criticism by IOs, INGOs and liberal states, the repressive state will start to make *tactical concessions.* In most cases these are low cost concessions like showing greater tolerance for demonstrations or releasing a few political prisoners. But through these concessions inner advocacy groups can become stronger and the pressure to meet expectations grows even stronger. As a result, the *boomerang effect* eventuates.

Fourth, the effort by the transnational network begins to make a dent and gives rise to a policy change (or, also possible, a regime change). At the beginning, the repressive regime begins to sign relevant international human rights treaties and start to build up and strengthen domestic human rights groups, laws and institutions. With these actions the state shows commitment to human rights norms. This step is called *prescriptive status.*

1 This procedure is called *boomerang effect* or *boomerang pattern.* It was invented by *Keck* and *Sikkink* (1998) and has been included in the spiral model. It describes the process of NGOs bypassing "their states and directly search[ing] out international allies to try to bring pressure on their states from outside. This is most obviously the case in human rights campaigns. [...] issues where governments are inaccessible or deaf to groups whose claims may nonetheless resonate elsewhere, international contacts can amplify the demands of domestic groups, pry open space for new issues, and then echo back these demands into the domestic arena" (Keck & Sikkink 1998: 12 f.).

In the last step, the state changes its actual behavior to the point of sustained compliance with international human rights norms and can become a human rights advocate itself. This phase is named *rule-consistent behavior.*

During all of these steps, there are four modes of social action that the transnational advocacy network can carry out to enforce the development of a repressive state into a state of rule-consistent behavior[2] (Risse et al. 2013: 12ff.). First of all, *coercion* can be used to make a state comply with a norm. Two ways are possible: military and legal enforcement. Whereas military coercion is against the will of the repressing state, the state subjugated itself voluntarily to a legal regime, e.g., the *International Criminal Court* (ICC). The more legal regimes that exist in order to enforce human right issues, the more legal measures will be applied in place of military force.

Second, *changing incentives* can change a state's behavior. These incentives can be positive or negative. While negative incentives, like sanctions, are used to punish non-compliance, positive incentives, like foreign aid, can be used to encourage compliance.[3]

Persuasion and discourse are two other tools of enforcing human right norms. Through arguing, persuasion and learning tactics the repressing state may be convinced of the legitimacy of the norm. Also, the process of naming and shaming falls into this category. An advantage of this method is that it is probably one of the most sustainable. On the other hand, a policy change by a repressing state is rarely based on pure persuasion alone. This method is often combined with other measures.

Last but not least, *capacity building* can also be used to enhance human rights norms. This applies mainly to states that cannot exercise full sovereignty over their territory (limited statehood). In this case, all other tools are completely ineffective, because even if the repressive state chose to support human right norms, it could not comply with these norms (involuntary non-compliance).

2 The modes of social action have been extended in the revised approach. The original framework employs mainly discursive measures.

3 The effectiveness of positive incentives is contentious. In one of the first empirical studies on this topic, Nielsen and Simmons (2015) can find no evidence for rising benefits after the ratification of human rights treaties.

Furthermore, Risse et al. (2013: 16ff.) outlined certain scope conditions under which compliance with human right norms is more likely. This was done in the revised version due to the fact that the scholars had to explain why big and powerful states, like China and the USA, in addition to other states, still do not comply fully with human right norms. These five scope conditions are: regime type, state capacity, rule implementation, material vulnerability and social vulnerability.

First, it matters whether the relevant state is a democracy or not. Non-democratic regimes are less likely to comply with human rights. Second, it is an issue if the statehood is consolidated or limited. As mentioned above, limited statehood can be one of the reasons why a state does not implement certain norms. Third, a decentralized rule implementation (which means that for an implementation of norms and rules different, decentralized – often estranged – actors have to come to an agreement) makes a rule-consistent behavior less likely. Fourth, the vulnerability of a state to external and international pressures influences the rule compliance (material vulnerability). This implies that states with strong economic and military resources are less vulnerable to certain rule enforcing measures. Fifth, a state's social vulnerability matters. The bigger the state's desire to be a member of the international human rights society, the stronger the vulnerability to discursive measures like naming and shaming. In addition, a counter-discourse can be set by the repressing state to challenge the discursive pressures (for example, in Asia and to a certain degree in the West itself).

In sum, the updated version of the spiral model matches today's occurrences much better. As Risse et al. (2013: 4) allow, the first version was very positivistic and mainly driven by a discursive approach based on the Habermas's discourse theory. The modes of social action were primarily based on persuasion of a non-complying state. With the second, revised, version, the scholars also included *realistic* measures to enforce compliance, like coercion and incentives, to the spiral model. Furthermore, they equipped the framework with conditions that can explain why the adoption of human right norms has stalled in some cases.

Hence, the spiral model cannot only be used to explain the diffusion of human rights norms. Using the revised version, the question why norm adoption in some cases comes to a standstill can be explained. But is this framework also appropriate for explaining the derogation of a rule-consistent behavior? Sikkink (2013) performed the first analysis by exploring the torture practices of the USA in Guantanamo and elsewhere. According to her, the US violations of the *Convention against Torture* were possible because the USA invoked a counter discourse advocating the norm of security (Sikkink (2013) calls it *anti-terror norm*). This new norm made the US government less vulnerable because many parts of the US population as well as many US allies accepted it. In addition to the lack of social vulnerability, she holds that the material vulnerability of the USA is low as well. These factors protected the USA from national and international pressure. This is why the spiral model would not work. Nevertheless, she concludes that the spiral model would not fit the US torture case completely, because "the spiral model suggests that a prescriptive status phase of treaty ratification usually follows the state of tactical concessions" (Sikkink 2013: 162) and not the other way around. However, she did not think about amending the spiral model in a way to explain these occurrences.

In this paper, another attempt shall be made to explain the derogation of a human rights norm, in this case privacy, with the spiral model. In order to do so, the privacy norm has to be highlighted with the objective to determine what is meant by privacy. This topic will be discussed in the following chapter.

3. Norm Diffusion: How Privacy Became an International Norm

A vast number of attempts have been made to define privacy.[4] A multitude of approaches show that it is impossible to define privacy straight to the point. Although privacy is often seen as a vague concept, it has become important all over the world (Solove 2008: 1 f.). Helen Nissenbaum (2010: 129ff.) tried to overcome the *overtheorization* of privacy, using an approach of contextual integrity. She holds that privacy is

> a right to live in a world in which our expectations about the flow of personal information are, for the most part, met; expectations that are shaped not only by force of habit and connection but a general confidence in the mutual support these flows accord to key principles of social life, including moral and political ones. […] [This approach to privacy] builds on the substantive thesis that more-or-less coherent, distinctive systems of norms, which shape the contours of our expectations, evolve within the distinctive contexts that make up the social. (Nissenbaum 2010: 231 f.)

This concept overcomes the traditional static frameworks of privacy, which consist mainly of four popular concepts: the definition of privacy in terms of non-interference, limited accessibility, informational control and of intimate or sensitive aspects of persons' life (Bygrave 2010: 170). One definition that considers all of these spheres has been established by Beate Rössler (2001). She classifies privacy into three different spheres: decisional privacy (defense of room to maneuver and decision against unwanted influence of others; similar to the non-interference approach), informational privacy (to control the knowledge of others about personal information of oneself; similar to the infor-

4 It goes beyond the scope of this paper to illustrate every possible theoretical definition of privacy, and it is also not the target of this chapter to provide it. Good starting points to get an overview of the theoretical approaches to privacy are provided by Solove (2002 & 2008), Solove and Schwartz (2009: 39ff.) and Nissenbaum (2010: 67ff., 89ff.).

mational control approach), and local privacy (a physical place of retreat, e.g., the home; similar to the limited accessibility and sensitive aspects approach) (Rössler 2001: 144ff.). As a matter of course, in view of today's technical development, the second sphere is the most important dimension of privacy (Schiedermair 2012: 12) – especially in regard to the Snowden revelations.

To view privacy as the control of personal information is an approach that has its roots in the era of upcoming data protection. The founding father of this concept, Alan Westin (1970), frames privacy as "the claim of individuals, groups, or institutions to determine for themselves when, how and to what extent information about them is communicated to others" (7). In a broader sense, the reference of accessibility is something very important to the definition of privacy, which Altmann (1977) highlights, as he describes privacy as "the selective control of access to the self, […] whereby people can make themselves accessible or inaccessible to others" (67ff.). As a result, in this paper privacy is defined as the control of access to the self and the flow of personal information with regard to the contextual expectation of privacy.

This is only a broad philosophical definition. However, this vagueness is necessary to cover the social change of what types of things are expected to be private. Depending on the changing relationship between the individual and the state, the term privacy is fashioned by social transformation (Schiedermair 2012: 8). On the following pages, it is important to take a closer look at the development of privacy as a social norm, a juridical norm and an international norm.

3.1. Privacy as Social Norm

The roots of privacy as a norm of social life date back to antiquity and can be found for the first time in history in old Jewish laws dating back more than 2000 years (Diffie & Landau 2012: 142).[5] Early on, they em-

5 The etymological roots of the word *privacy* date back to antiquity as well. Already the Latin term *privatus* means *apart from the state* (Ennöckl 2014: 15). At the same time, the Romans created the word *publicus*, which later on became the basis for the term *publicity*, the counterpart of privacy (Schiedermair 2012: 27).

phasized that the individual's freedom to speak and act was already limited if someone assumed, but did not know, that she was monitored (Schmale & Tinnefeld 2014: 83). Within the musings of the first philosophers of the Western world, the idea of privacy was present. Aristotle drew a separating line between the public sphere, *polis*, and the household, *oikos*. This distinction was adopted by the Romans, who were among the first who differentiated between a *ius publicum* and a *ius privatum* (which are the origins of contemporary public and private law) (Schiedermair 2012: 24ff.).

But unlike contemporary views on privacy, the ancient concept of privacy held that the place of freedom and self-fulfillment was the public sphere and not the private one. The polis is the area where all citizens manage the political matters of the society free and equal. It was the place where citizens could develop their virtues and gain social reputation. The assumption of a public office was considered as the "perfection of human being" (Ennöckl 2014: 16). On the contrary, the household was the sphere of necessity, and people could only develop to the full in the public sphere. This point of view – the private sphere as burdensome, the public as something positive – has influenced Western philosophy until today (Ennöckl 2014: 16; Schiedermair 2012: 25).

The abstract concepts of privacy and publicity that had been held in ancient times also influenced life in medieval times, although the governmental system changed dramatically. The hierarchical structure of the *oikos* was transferred to the political order. Hence, Schiedermair rightly speaks of the "privatization of power" (2012: 29).[6] Nevertheless, the public sphere was diminished but not dead. At that time, the word *publicus* described everything that was related to power, and it has survived in many forms, e.g., as *persona publica* (person who represents the interests of society) (Schiedermair 2012: 28ff.). However, the ancient meaning of *private* as something that is not related to public issues blurred, because public matters were handled in a private way whereas *public* was still something related to the power of the monarch.

6 How important private relationships became, particularly with regard to the family, can be seen in the formation of family arms at that time (Schiedermair 2012: 30).

The next big change in the denotation of the private and public spheres came with the Renaissance. People changed their worldview from a theocentric to an anthropocentric one; the individual was discovered and became increasingly important. This development paved the way for the contemporary understanding of privacy because it gave rise to an appreciation of the private sphere that had never existed before.

The emergence of ways to express individuality increased in many ways. Portraits and biographies became popular while chronicles were being written for the first time. This was a trend that was not only observed in Europe but also in China, Japan and in the Islamic world (Schiedermair 2012: 31 f.). On the spatial level, individualism was expressed through the establishment of rooms in houses. Lockable bedrooms and bathrooms were created, and individuals got their own rooms. Whereas in the Middle Ages loneliness was only common during prayers and was otherwise considered as detrimental, this point of view changed in the late 17th century. In times of Enlightenment, this new worldview continued to influence the everyday life of people. Rooms were decorated with personal belongings and were seen as an expression of the person who lived in that room. Self-reflection became common and was practiced by keeping a journal, interpreting dreams and confessing. In the 18th and 19th centuries, the blooming of individuality was expressed by the use of prenames (Schiedermair 2012: 30ff.).

The significant historical events at that time were the French Revolution and the *Declaration of the Rights of Man and of the Citizen* in 1789, which marked the birth of the idea of universal rights. The declaration included, among others, the right to freedom (freedom of action) and the freedom of religion. These rights, therefore, opposed the absolutistic state, which wielded influence to every sphere of human life. Although it would take another 100 years until the first approach to the right to privacy was launched, the claims of the declaration's rights are not imaginable without a conceptual prerequisite of a private sphere. To claim these rights implies a differentiation between a public sphere, which is also the sphere of the state, and a private sphere, which belongs to the individual alone and precedes the state (Ennöckl 2014: 18 f.; Schiedermair 2012: 34). This differentiation led to a new development: The private sphere is now considered to be an individual sphere. In medieval times, privacy could be pretty much associated with family life, with its organizational structure transferred to the political order. After 1789, fundamental rights claimed to acknowledge a sphere that belonged only to the individual. This idea was reflected in many constitutions in the 19th century. Although not one guaranteed a right to privacy, they contained rights that we consider today as something included to the right to privacy. This applies to the householder's right and to the privacy of correspondence (letters)[7] (Ennöckl 2014: 18).

Important for the further development of the term privacy is the inversion of *Aristotle's* paradigm. No longer was the public sphere the place where the individual develops. The place for self-development shifted to the private sphere. In England, *privacy* became a synonym for a happy, middle-class way of life that is best expressed by the phrase *my home is my castle*. Furthermore, in Germany people also turned towards privacy: Disappointed by the political developments (Restauration), the *Biedermeier* age set in, and people experienced happiness in their private spheres (Schiedermair 2012: 35 f.).

While the origins of privacy are rooted in occidental philosophy and European developments led to the individualization of privacy and to the creation of privacy as the social norm we know today, the actual *right to privacy* was invented in the USA, as the following section exhibits.

7 The USA was not excluded from this development, either. In 1710, the British government established the first postal delivery system in the USA and, at the same time, created the first privacy protection for letters: they were just allowed to be opened with a permission of the secretary of state (at least in theory). After the independence of the USA, Congress adopted the first Postal Act that prohibited postal officials to open mails. In 1825, Congress adopted the second Postal Act that generally prohibited prying into another person's mail. Unfortunately, people did not follow the law and in times of Civil War even government officials tried to open private mail. In 1878, the Supreme Court ruled that a search warrant is necessary for the government to open mail (Diffie & Landau 2007: 144ff.).

3.2. Privacy as Juridical Norm

It took until the end of the 19th century for privacy to become a legal norm. This was only possible through the previous developments, which lead to the emergence of individuality leading the way.

In December 1890, Boston lawyers Samuel D. Warren and Louis D. Brandeis published an article named *The Right to Privacy*. This moment is generally seen as the birth of a modern understanding of privacy and it is still considered to be "the most important article ever written about privacy" (Solove & Schwartz 2009: 10). The changes of social life in the USA paved the way for the development of the right to privacy: an stupendously growing population including a fundamental change of living conditions due to urbanization that resulted in a less segregated life; technological developments including the invention of photography and snap cameras, making it possible for any individual to take pictures everywhere and at any time; and the proliferation of newspapers, which became affordable for everyone and which led to the evolution of the so-called *yellow press* that reported about famous and rich people's lives (Glancy 1979: 7ff.; Solove & Schwartz 2009: 10ff.).

Both Warren and Brandeis wanted to adapt the law to the modern challenges. From their point of view, it was an old principle of common law "that the individual shall have full protection in person and in property [...], but it has been found necessary from time to time to define anew the exact nature and extent of such protection" (Warren & Brandeis 1890: 1939). At that time, society was discussing the problem of pictures being taken without the consent of the photographed people and also the reporting of gossip and rumors in the newspapers without the consent of the injured. The problem was that the law did not provide any protection against this.

In the 19th century, one very common way of protecting ones privacy in the USA was to sue people for criminal libel.[8] But unfortunately for the claimant the courts accepted the truth as a defense against

8 At that time, libel was defined in the USA as "malicious defamations of any person [...] made public by either printing, writing, signs, or pictures, in order to provoke him to wrath, or expose him to public hatred, contempt, and ridicule" (Glancy 1979: 12).

criminal libel. If the truth of the libel could be proven, then malicious intent was disproven, which was necessary for the finding of criminal libel. The opinion that everything that is true is also allowed to be said and printed was also an argument made by many in the public debate to defend the activity of the *yellow press* (Glancy 1979: 10ff.).

Therefore they invented the right to privacy that was based on *the right to be let alone*, a phrase invented by the judge Thomas Cooley (Glancy 1979: 3 f.). According to Warren and Brandeis, there had been several problems with the state of the law. First, the law of libel would deal only with damage to reputation regarding the external relations of an individual, but it did not protect the injury of the individual's own feelings. There would be no remedy for mental suffering. Second, they felt that the right to property should extend to happenings in the domestic circle. Their argument is based on the – already present at that time – existing protection of thoughts. No one could be forced to express his thoughts or sentiments. Also poems, letters and diary entries would be protected, wholly independent of possessing the material (e.g. paper) on which it is written (Warren & Brandeis 1890: 197ff.). This right would only be lost if the author decided to publish his thoughts. Hence, they concluded that

> […] the protection afforded to thoughts, sentiments, and emotions, expressed through the medium of writing or of the arts, so far as it consists in preventing publication, is merely an instance of the enforcement of the more general right of the individual to be let alone. […] The principle which protects personal writings and all other personal productions, not against theft and physical appropriation, but against publication in any form, is in reality not the principle of private property, but that of an inviolate personality. (Warren & Brandeis 1890: 205)

So they argued that this right of personality needed to be extended to things happening in the domestic circle to adjust this right to contemporary times and claims of society. With it they hold that the individual determines what is considered private, and hence they do not follow previous approaches of determining privacy as something bound to the local sphere (e.g., the home). By conceptualizing privacy as something that guarantees the inviolate personality, it calls for the individual to define his own private sphere (Ennöckl 2014: 20).

Hence, what Warren and Brandeis did was nothing more than defining the common basis of present rights. This common principle is the right to privacy. They hold that the right to privacy is nothing more than the foundation of all existing laws to prevent an intrusion into the personality, which is part of the right to life. Now it had to be adjusted to modern times:

> The principle which protects personal writings and any other productions of the intellect or of the emotions, is the right to privacy, and the law has no new principle to formulate when it extends this protection to the personal appearance, sayings, acts, and to personal relation, domestic or otherwise. (Warren &Brandeis 1890: 213)

With this invention of a legal theory for the right to privacy, they protected the social norm of privacy[9] from disappearing in a technological world. For a very long time, privacy was a fact of life. Through technical developments, it was something that could hardly have been achieved by individuals on their own from the 19th century on. Instead, privacy is now something controlled by societies (or governments, respectively) that can guarantee or deny this norm. Consequently, we can observe the opposite trend during medieval times: While the public sphere became privatized in the Middle Ages, it was now extended to private issues increasingly. Many people perceived this as wrong, but there was no clear juridical concept that could be employed in this situation. The existing concepts and causes of action hit the wall and did not offer adequate protection of the private sphere. With the approach that considers the right to privacy as a part of the inviolate personality, Warren and Brandeis offered a way out and both rescued the norm of privacy in a technological age and transferred the social norm into a legal concept.

With this article, Warren and Brandeis activated a juridical debate about the right to privacy, which was essential for the creation of a fundamental right to privacy in the UDHR more than half a century later (Ennöckl 2014: 20 f.). However, the article did not have an immediate influence on the jurisdiction (Prosser 1960: 384 f.). It took more than a decade until the first court decisions, which acknowledged a right to

9 As a matter of course, Warren and Brandeis also provided limitations to the right to privacy. According to them, this right could not be used to prohibit publications of public interest; nor should it be used to prevent publications in public bodies (like courts, municipal assemblies) (Warren & Brandeis 1890: 214ff.).

privacy, could be found in the states of New York and Georgia (Solove & Schwartz 2009: 26; Prosser 1960: 385).[10]

As a matter of course, technological progress continued to challenge the right to privacy. In 1928, the first case was brought to the US Supreme Court where the judges had to decide about the legality of wiretapping. Ironically, Brandeis was one of the judges in this case involving businessmen Roy Olmstead. To convict him of illegal liquor distribution, federal agents wiretapped the phone line of his headquarters. Later, those wiretap tapes played a crucial role in court. The matter of particular interest was whether those tapes could be valid in court. They were obtained without a warrant, but a warrant was actually only necessary for entering into private homes or offices (as the Fourth Amendment dictated). The Supreme Court ruled that the wiretaps were legal without a warrant, but the judge Brandeis published a dissent:[11]

> The protection guaranteed by the Amendments is much broader in scope. [...] They recognized the significance of man's spiritual nature, of his feelings and his intellect. [...] They sought to protect Americans in their beliefs, their thoughts, their emotions and their sensations. [...] To protect that right, every unjustifiable intrusion by the Government upon privacy of the individual, whatever the means employed, must be deemed a violation of the Fourth Amendment. (Cited in Diffie & Landau 2007: 149 f.)

It took one more decade until the Supreme Court followed the argumentation of Brandeis and ruled, in 1937, that wiretapping was illegal. Further judgments confirmed this point of view (Diffie & Landau 2007: 150).[12]

---

10 An overview of the first privacy tort cases by Prosser (1960) epitomized the spread of the judicial norm of privacy in the USA in a very good way.

11 With this decision the Supreme Court judged against the public opinion. Eavesdropping – although conducted for a law enforcement purpose – was not accepted by most Americans. Even Republicans were concerned about this judgment. When the philosopher Nicolas Murray Butler defended the Supreme Court's decision at the congress of the Republican Party, he was catcalled (Kammerer 2015: 30).

12 One of these judgements was Katz vs. United States in 1967, when the Supreme Court ruled: "[A]n enclosed telephone booth is an area where, like a home, [...] a person has a constitutionally protected reasonable expectation of privacy" (cited in Mills 2015: 198 f.).
Even though the influence of the Warren and Brandeis article on the jurisdiction in the USA is well examined in the research literature, this is, in the cold light of the

Through the upcoming abilities to interfere with one's privacy by use of wiretapping, technical inventions also tried to secure man's privacy among the juridical possibilities of resistance. At the beginning of the 20th century, voice scramblers were introduced. Furthermore, the upcoming World War II accelerated the development of the first bug proof telephone, *Sigsaly*, by the US military in the 1940 s. Unfortunately, it did not go a long way towards bettering the protection of ordinary people's privacy. It was so expensive that only two people in the world could afford such devices: Roosevelt and Churchill (Diffie & Landau 2007: 61 f.; Weadon 2009).

All in all, one can observe that the 19th and the first half of the 20th century were crucial to establishing a right to privacy. Thus, the social norm of privacy was cast in the legislative mold. The next step of privacy becoming an international norm including a human rights regime that aims to protect this norm began after World War II.

3.3. Privacy as International Norm

Whereas the invention of the right to privacy occurred in the USA, European countries mainly initiated the development of privacy as an international norm, especially with regard to data protection.

At the very beginning, the cruel wrongdoings of Nazi Germany and Stalinism brought to mind that in functioning democratic societies the citizens need a certain degree of freedom from the state (Ennöckl 2014: 20). That is why one of the very first targets of the United Nations (UN) was the protection of human rights (Schiedermair 2012: 60). In 1946, a human rights commission was appointed, headed by Eleanor Roosevelt, to develop an *International Bill of Rights* composed of a legally unbinding UDHR and the two legally binding covenants, the *International Covenant on Economic, Social and Cultural Rights* (ICESCR) and the *International Covenant on Civil and Political*

day, not the case in Europe. How exactly the right to privacy made his way to Europe, is not explained in detail by contemporary research literature and remains an academic void. The same applies to the question how, when and why the norm of privacy was added to the claims made by human rights advocates. This has to be the subject of further research.

Rights (ICCPR) (Schiedermair 2012: 62). The right to privacy is also covered by these international agreements and was established as a fundamental right.

In the first draft of the UDHR, the right to privacy was already mentioned. The *June 1947 Human Rights Commission Draft* states: "The privacy of the home and of correspondence and respect for reputation shall be protected by law" (cited in Glendon 2002: 283). While the course of discussion first led to a close connection of the right to privacy to the right to property and seizures, this connection became loosened over time. That features the personal dimension of privacy to a larger extent and detaches it from a material meaning (like a house). Hence, Article 12 of the UDHR states: "No one shall be subjected to arbitrary interference with his privacy, family, home or correspondence, nor to attacks upon his honour and reputation. Everyone has the right to the protection of the law against such interference or attacks" (United Nations n.d.). As a matter of course, informational privacy is not mentioned by the UDHR. But the fact that the personal dimension of privacy was strengthened by this formulation makes today's privacy activists claim that the private sphere also covers the informational dimension (Schiedermair 2012: 65). In any case, with that development privacy became a fundamental human right (Solove 2008: 3 f.).

With the UDHR, the human rights were for the first time recognized at the international level (Abu-Laban 2014: 422). The acknowledgment specifically applies to the right to privacy. When the UN General Assembly had a vote on the UDHR in 1948, it was proposed to ballot for every article separately. The vote for Article 12 was unanimous (Schiedermair 2012: 66).

In 1966, the ICCPR was adopted. The right to privacy continued to play a major role and was perpetuated in Article 17. During the discussion by the members of the human rights commission about the protection of privacy, all agreed to the necessity of the enshrinement of the right to privacy. This shows that all states generally agreed to the protection of everyone's privacy as a universal human right (Schiedermair 2012: 72 f.). Nevertheless, certain human rights can be derogated in case of public emergency. This is in fact allowed by the ICCPR. Only the right to life and the right not be subjected to torture are indispensable (Chesterman 2011: 44 f.).

With the enshrining of privacy as a human right, this norm was finally an international norm. From then on, IOs played a major role in the conservation and the advancement of the norm of privacy. Most notably, the UN, the Organization for Economic Co-Operation and Development (OECD), the Council of Europe (CoE) and the EU achieved the most to adopt the norm of privacy to further technological developments – which challenged privacy enormously with the invention of computers and the Internet.

In 1968, the participants of the International UN Conference on Human Rights in Teheran already noticed that technological development could have not only positive outcomes for human rights. Especially with regard to the respect for privacy and the protection of human personality, they recommended research on the implications of technical developments on human rights. The UN General Assembly reacted immediately and in the same year adopted resolution 2450, which opines that the

> General Assembly, […] sharing the concern of the Conference that recent scientific discoveries and technological advances […] may […] endanger the rights and freedoms of individuals […], invites the Secretary-General to undertake […] a study of the problems […], in particular [regarding the] respect for privacy of individuals […]. (United Nations General Assembly 1968)

This was the first time that the UN General Assembly concerned itself with the protection of privacy in the upcoming digital age (Schiedermair 2012: 120).[13] Thereby, they followed the zeitgeist. At that time technological development was mainly characterized by three trends. First, information was starting to be digitalized. Hence, more personal

13 In the sequel, the UN published many reports regarding this topic. One of the most influential was the *Study of the Relevant Guidelines in the Field of Computerized Personal Files* by Special Rapporteur Louis Joinet, which paved the way for the *Guidelines for the Regulation of Computerized Personal Data Files,* adopted by the UN in 1990. Those non-binding guidelines are one of the most important documents by the UN regarding privacy in the digital age. Albeit the intention was to encourage member states lacking data protection laws to enact such laws, the influence of this guideline was limited compared to similar activities by other IOs (Bygrave 2010: 184 f.; Schiedermair 2012: 120ff.).

information could be collected more easily. Second, the technical devices got smaller (miniaturization), a process accompanied by decentralization. Thus, the use of digitalized personal information was increasing enormously, and it was also easier to obtain such information. Third, networking made personal information accessible all over the globe. Some of these characteristics had been inherent in the technical development over time, but now these processes accelerated (Ennöckl 2014: 7ff.).

Finally, it was the invention of computers that brought privacy to mind, starting with public discussions in the USA in the 1960 s about how personal information should be processed and how privacy could be obtained under these new circumstances (Bygrave 2010: 167). The offending object was the proposal for a centralized databank containing census data in the USA in 1966 (Bennett 1992: 46). Later, the center of the question was the allocation of consumer credit and, subsequently, record keeping by government authorities, which was brought up by the Watergate scandal (Rule 2014: 66). In the USA and in the UK as well, study commissions were constituted to investigate what outcomes those new developments would have and how the countries should react to it (Regan 2014: 401). Thus, the same discussion that hit the USA was also present in Europe (Bygrave 2010: 167), and an answer was demanded, leading to the creation of *data protection*[14] in the

14 *Data protection* is a term whose origins go back to the German word *Datenschutz*. It is mostly used in European countries whereas outside Europe scholars refer to terms like *protection of privacy, data privacy,* or *information privacy*. In this paper, I will employ the term *data protection,* unless I acknowledge that it has weaknesses as well. On the one hand, *data protection* hides the actual interest at stake (which is privacy), but, on the other hand, it allows a much better differentiation between the informational and, e.g., the physical dimension of the term privacy.
Moreover, data protection cannot only be related to privacy. Most notably in the Scandinavian discussion about privacy the insight arose that the demand for data protection is not only determined by the interest in privacy. Also values, like a citizen friendly administration, the proportionality of control and the rule of law can call for data protection laws (Bygrave 2010: 166, 168 f., 172 f.).

1970 s. Thus, the principles of privacy were transferred to the digital sphere.[15]

All states faced the occurrence of digital data procession, making the responses converge to a certain degree, although national forces contributed to local variations (Bennett 1992: 221ff.). This development "made privacy erupt into a frontline issue around the world" (Solove 2008: 4).

The history of data protection began in 1970, when the first data protection law in the world was adopted in Wiesbaden, the capital of the German federal state of Hesse.[16] Many countries[17] and German states followed this approach and adopted similar laws and regulations (Schwartz 2013: 1966). A few years later, in 1983, data protection was granted the stance of a fundamental right by the German Federal Constitutional Court. The court created the principle of *informational self-determination*. According to the Constitutional Court, everyone has the right to be in charge of the disclosure of personal information and how one's personal data is used in cases of disclosure (Garstka 2003: 48). With this principle, the right to privacy, the right to decide about the access to the self, was carried forward to the digital sphere. Later, the right to informational self-determination became a key principle in the data protection approach of the EU and many European countries.

15 In the academic discussion, data protection is viewed as the continuance of the social norm of privacy (Schmale 2014: 79 f.). Nevertheless, contrary opinions still find their way into newspapers, arguing that privacy was a very new phenomenon whose complete disappearance in a digital world would not really matter (Schariatmadari 2015). As this chapter shows, this point of view is more than dubious.

16 At that time the initiation of a data protection law was seen as a step to protect personal freedom. The then minister-president of Hessen, Albert Osswald, viewed that law as a step to the next decade and as a necessity to defend the country against developments imagined by the novelist *George Orwell:* "Die Orwellsche Vision des allwissenden Staates, der die intimsten Winkel menschlicher Lebenssphäre ausforscht, wird in unserem Land nicht Wirklichkeit werden" (Der Spiegel 1971: 88).

17 Sweden (1973), Austria, Denmark, France and Norway (all 1978) adopted data protection laws as well. The first federal German law regarding data protection was adopted in 1977 (Schwartz 2013: 1969).

Because the emerging flow of data was not bound to borders, international agreements were inevitable. Already in the late 1960 s, the OECD held meetings and international conferences to tackle the problems the new international data flow implicated (Schiedermair 2012: 172 f.). The OECD first broke the ground in 1980 with her *Guidelines Governing the Protection of Privacy and Transborder Flows of Personal Data*, "the first international statement of essential information privacy principles" (Schwartz 2013: 1966). The guideline contains in their preface a statement concerning the human right to privacy minded to prevent "violations of fundamental human rights, such as the unlawful storage of personal data, the storage of inaccurate personal data, or the abuse or unauthorized disclosure of such data" (Organization for Economic Co-Operation and Development 1980), although one main factor for adopting the guidelines was the economic necessity of the free flow of data (Schwartz 2013: 1971). To obtain this target, the individual, according to the guideline, should have the right to obtain the information from a data controller if information about this person has been saved and what kind of information is saved. Furthermore, everyone should have the right to challenge this information and, if successful, can be adamant that the data are deleted or modified. In addition to that, the data collection should have legal limits; also an earmarking should be established (Organization for Economic Co-Operation and Development 1980). Albeit these guidelines were non-binding, they influenced national legislation of OECD member states and non-member states (Schwartz 2013: 1970; Schiedermair 2012: 151).

Just one year later, in 1981, the CoE launched the world's first legally binding guidelines on data protection. Contrary to the OECD, whose approach is also based on an economic approach, the CoE guidelines focus on human rights. This is due to the fact that the CoE convention on data protection drew inspiration directly from the *European Convention of Human Rights*, which was adopted in 1950 by the CoE. In Article 12, it entails a right to privacy: "Everyone has the right to respect for his private and family life, his home and his correspondence" (Council of Europe n.d.: 10).

Already in the late 1960 s the CoE recognized a potential threat to human rights by automatic data processing. The CoE members initiated a study on adequate privacy protection in times of technological development, which concluded that most of the national laws at that time did not provide sufficient protection. Albeit the result of this were two non-binding resolutions on data protection adopted by the CoE in the 1970 s, it was clear to many CoE experts that a binding international agreement would be inevitable to achieve a satisfactory protection. A committee of experts on data processing was constituted that would, in close cooperation with the OECD, work out a draft for a convention. After a revision of this draft, the council of ministers adopted the *Convention for the Protection of Individuals with regard to Automatic Processing of Personal Data* in January 1981 (Schiedermair 2012: 316ff.; Ennöckl 2014: 313ff.). It contains a clear acknowledgement to "everyone's rights and fundamental freedoms, and in particular the right to the respect for privacy [...] recognising that it is necessary to reconcile the fundamental values of the respect for privacy and the free flow of information between peoples" (Council of Europe 1981).

The convention influenced the further developments of data protection considerably. On the one hand, it affected many countries around the world (Schwartz 2013: 1967). This is not too surprising considering the fact that experts from many countries – including the USA, Canada, Japan and Australia – contributed to the expert committee, which finalized the draft of the convention (Schiedermair 2012: 318). On the other hand, this international agreement set five basic principles that have shaped the European data protection until today. First, personal data have to be obtained and processed in a lawful way. Second, personal data should just be stored and used for the specific purposes they were collected for. Third, they have to meet this purpose. Fourth, the personal information has to be correct and up to date. Furthermore, it should not be possible to identify the individual *(data owner)* by this data longer than necessary (Ennöckl 2014: 315).

In the 1990 s, a new major player entered the stage of data protection: the EU. This was a time of increasing economic activity between EU member states accompanied by high demands for personal information. To avoid damaging the economic prosperity with national regulations on data protection, the EU adopted a data protection directive in 1995. The directive aimed to both ensure a high and equal level of protection of "fundamental rights and freedoms of natural persons, and in particular their right to privacy" (European Union 1995) in the

EU and to facilitate and enhance the flow of personal information between states. But this directive was not only groundbreaking for EU members; its influence was considerable on the whole world because of its extraterritorial approach: The directive prohibits data transfers to states outside of the EU that have no adequate level of data protection. "This restriction [...] reflects an underlying belief that personal information of EU citizens merits protection throughout the world and not merely within the EU" (Schwartz 2013: 1973). It was the rise of a uniform legislation in terms of data protection not only in the EU but also in the world, because other countries followed the EU approach and not the path of the US (Schwartz 2013: 1979). This development prompted Rule (2014) to speak of a "global 'privacy club'" (67) that continues to increase membership figures: "Except in the United States, national privacy codes establish not just a body of law and policy for institutional treatment of personal information, but also a national privacy commissioner and a small staff to uphold the law and advocate privacy values in the public forum" (67).

While the EU adopted a civil liberties approach to handle the problems of digitalization, the USA decided to choose another option based on the accountability and responsibility of the data collecting organizations (see next part of this chapter; Regan 2014: 398). But as a matter of course, also the USA should – theoretically – match the standards of European legislation to process personal information about European citizens. That is why the USA and the EU started to negotiate the Safe Harbor agreement in 1998. With it, not every member state of the EU has to approve the data flow to the USA, which makes data transfer easier. Even though the EU had never officially considered the US approach as insufficient, first doubts about the sufficient data protection in the USA came up already in 1999. Although the European Parliament rejected the agreement in a non-binding decision, the European Commission adopted the arrangement (Schwartz 2013:1979ff.). It took 15 years until the European Court of Justice declared this agreement invalid in the light of the Snowden revelations (Gibbs 2015).

The march of privacy through the IOs was considerably successful. It was accompanied by the development of privacy (I)NGOs, although the history of a modern approach to privacy seems to be quite elitist. From the invention of the right to privacy by a Boston upper-class lawyer to the spread of the norm of privacy in the 1960 s and 1970 s through the support of the concept of data protection by many academics, this perspective seems to be fairly true (Rule 2014: 66). Even so, privacy has become a social movement in the last decades of the 20th century (Bennett 2011: 310 f.). The same discussion that set the stage for IOs to enhance the norm of privacy was causal for the creation of a non-governmental movement for privacy (mainly through NGOs)[18] although their composition is different from the classical social movements (Rule 2014: 66). First of all, there are just a few advocate groups that are barely interested in privacy. *Privacy International*[19], the *Electronic Frontier Foundation* (EFF)[20] and the *Electronic Privacy Information Center* (EPIC)[21] are a few examples. Other groups that are interested in the advocacy of privacy are civil rights and human rights groups like the *American Civil Liberties Union* (ACLU) or *Amnesty International* (AI). Furthermore, privacy has quite a long tradition in the business of consumer protection groups. All of these different groups

18 In general, that was the time of the development of human rights INGOs. In the 1970 s and 1980 s, they spread enormously and diversified (Keck & Sikkink 1998: 89ff.).

19 Founded in 1990, Privacy International was the first international human rights organization dealing solely with privacy issues. In 1998, they launched the *Big Brother Awards,* which are annually awarded to persons, organizations or companies that invaded people's privacy most. In February 2015, the London-based organization triumphed in court against the British intelligence agency GCHQ. Thanks to this judgement, individuals can now learn if the GCHQ holds information about them (Jansen 2015).

20 EFF is – according to self-description – the leading non-profit organization defending civil liberties in the digital world. Launched in San Francisco in 1990, it supports claimants in their efforts to try AT&T (telecommunication company) for their involvement in NSA spying activities (Electronic Frontier Foundation n.d.a).

21 EPIC is a public interest research centre in Washington, D.C. Established in 1994, it focuses on "emerging privacy and civil liberties issues and to protect privacy, freedom of expression, and democratic values in the information age" (Electronic Privacy Information Center n.d.). In 2014, they launched the *Champion of Freedom Award,* which is given to people or organizations that have safeguarded the right to privacy (Electronic Privacy Information Center n.d.).

have been somehow involved in Internet privacy issues.[22] They are considered to be the non-governmental privacy advocacy network. In the light of today's surveillance activities by the USA, it seems ironical that most advocacy groups sprouted in the US; they are also the most well funded ones (Bennett 2011: 301ff.). Scientists also played a very important role with regard to this movement. Through the invention of the concept of *public-key cryptography* by Whitfield Diffie, Martin Hellmann and Ralph Merkle in 1974, private, non-governmental encryption was made possible (Diffie & Landau 2007: 68).[23] From this point on, hackers also played a key role in the privacy movement. One example is the *Chaos Computer Club* (CCC), a German NGO with more than 5,000 members, mainly hackers, which was founded in 1981; and to their own account Europe's largest organization of hackers (Chaos Computer Club n.d.).

All in all, the non-governmental privacy advocacy network has not spread like other social movements. The main reason for this is a framing problem. First of all, privacy is a term that is not opposed by most people. In some ways, everyone can agree with the statement that a company or the state should not receive personal information that is not of their businesses. Because the topic is less controversial than others, there is no anti-movement (like, e.g., an anti-abortion movement). This is why the term privacy is not able to create any sense of collective

22 It is impossible – and beyond the scope of this chapter – to provide an entire list of all privacy advocacy groups and their activities. But at least Bennett (2011) provides a list of the main actors in privacy advocacy worldwide. Furthermore, there exist also other kinds of privacy protection that can hardly be studied scientifically. One example is the *everyday resistance*. This term describes individuals who try to beat or bypass surveillance systems in everyday life, which can be done for several reasons and by several approaches. But because one main characterization of this kind of *movement* is invisibility, it is hard to collect statistics on that. The main problem is that these people are not organized in a broader network or agree to a joint ideology and can therefore not be considered as belonging to a political movement. Nevertheless, their effort for privacy should not be withheld in this paper. Scholars expect anyhow that the space to carry out everyday resistance will get more restricted and regulated in the future (Gilliom & Monahan 2014: 405ff.).

23 The OECD also acknowledged the usefulness of encryption and encouraged the member states in 1997 to promote the use of cryptography to the end that it should help to "ensure the security of data, and to protect privacy, in national and global information and communications infrastructures, networks and systems" (Organization for Economic Co-Operation and Development 1997: 5).

identity. Furthermore, privacy is something that is of a highly contextual nature. It is, thus, very subjective: If people want to exercise their privacy rights or not, is to a very large part a subjective decision of an individual, which is, lastly, situation-dependent. Moreover, there exists no *go-big-or-go-home* decision relating to privacy; it is often balanced against other interests like national security, safety or the efficient conduct of marketing. One last point why privacy fails to serve as the determinant for a broad social movement is the absence of physical harm. It is very difficult to make harm – originated in a lack of privacy – visible to the public (Bennett 2011: 311 f.). Nevertheless, on another occasion, Bennett (2014: 418) holds that the privacy advocacy network will be more recognized in the future. Because of intensifying interactions in the network its visibility to the public should increase. Rules (2014), too, concludes that "the privacy protection movement has given rise to a still-unfolding global culture of concern over collection, sharing and use of personal information" (66).

In recent years, the privacy advocacy network has been well aware of possible threats to the right to privacy due to the progress of digitalization and potential surveillance practices. Hence, and because of the mounting proliferation of the security norm after 9/11, advocates have strengthened their effort to defend the right to privacy. First of all, NGOs have continued their work on privacy issues. One example is the *Madrid Privacy Declaration,* which was adopted in 2009 by a bulk of NGOs to call on governments to adjust their privacy and data protection laws, taking into account the danger of contemporary surveillance practices and possibilities (Bygrave 2010: 182).

The same is true of the IOs. The OECD revised their privacy guidelines – originally adopted in 1980 – in 2013. One of the amendments that the guideline notes is the following: "Exceptions to these Guidelines, including those relating to national sovereignty, national security and public policy ('ordre public'), should be: a) as few as possible, and b) made known to the public" (Organization for Economic Co-Operation and Development 2013: 14). Moreover, the OECD adopted a recommendation concerning the enforcement of privacy laws in 2007 and a report about the implementation of these laws in 2011 (Organization for Economic Co-Operation and Development 2013: 127ff.). They also initiated the *Global Privacy Enforcement Network*

(GPEN) in 2010, which has the function "to strengthen personal privacy protections in this global context by assisting public authorities with responsibilities for enforcing domestic privacy laws strengthen their capacities for cross-border cooperation" (Global Privacy Enforcement Network n.d.). Also the CoE revised the 1981 privacy guideline in 2001, again stating in the preamble that "with the increase in exchanges of personal data across national borders, it is necessary to ensure the effective protection of human rights and fundamental freedoms, and in particular the right to privacy" (Council of Europe 2001). The EU is no exception and has also strengthened the enforcement of privacy through the *Charter of Fundamental Rights of the European Union* (European Union 2012). Not only the right to privacy was adopted in this Charter, but also the right of the protection of personal data was cast in a seperate article. Article 8 governs the following:

> Everyone has the right to the protection of personal data concerning him or her. Such data must be processed fairly for specified purposes and on the basis of the consent of the person concerned or some other legitimate basis laid down by law. Everyone has the right of access to data which has been collected concerning him or her, and the right to have it rectified. (European Union 2012)

As one can see, privacy became an international norm in the 20th century, accepted by all UN member states as a fundamental human right. Until today, norm entrepreneurs have shown a considerable effort to uphold the norm of privacy and to pressure states to comply with it. Nevertheless – although the development of data protection pushed a European approach to privacy issues around the world – there is no consistent definition of privacy. As Zurawski (2015: 18ff.) notes, data protection cannot be equated with privacy. Whereas data protection is barely an expression of the power structure in a state (how the state has to handle the data of its citizens), privacy is a normative concept that is culturally different and that should be protected by data protection (Zurawski 2015: 18ff.). Even so, the understanding of privacy shapes the data protection approach enormously. The EU approach, for example, heavily underlies the self-determination approach that was shaped by the German Federal Constitutional Court. The same is true of the US, where a different understanding of privacy gave rise to a different data protection regime. The following part of this chapter will be devoted to these cultural nuances.

3.4. Cultural Differences: the USA and the EU

The right to privacy is mentioned in all regional human rights declarations in the world, albeit they differ in definition (Schiedermair 2012: 100ff.; Bygrave 2010: 190ff.). This is an expression of the diversity of this norm.[24] This section will focus on the differences between the EU and US approaches to privacy and data protection.

The US Constitution does not contain a right to privacy. However, it states several rights that protect the private sphere. So, the First Amendment contains the right to speak anonymously; the Third Amendment includes the protection of the home; and the Fourth Amendment protects people from warrantless and unreasonable searches and seizers of their persons, homes and letters (Solove & Schwartz 2009: 33 f.). [25] The most important amendment with regard to the right to privacy in communication issues is the Fourth Amend-

24 In all societies, privacy has been a necessary condition for human beings. "It seems that the ability to regulate interaction is necessary for individual and cultural survival, and unless people have figured out ways to control interaction, their status as intact human beings can well be in jeopardy" (Altmann 1977: 82). But as a matter of course, the degree of privacy of an individual has always been connected to the culture or society he or she lives in. According to Altmann (1977: 72ff.), the scale reaches from cultures of minimal privacy (like the Mehinacu culture, the Javanese culture or the culture of the Pygmies of Zaire) to cultures of maximal privacy (like the Balinese culture or the culture of the Muslim Tuareg), but there exists no culture in which the possibility of privacy is completely denied.
Nonetheless, a few main trajectories seem to apply in general. One main trajectory seems to apply to all countries: The more complex a society is, the bigger is the concern for privacy. Moore (1984, cited in Bygrave 2010: 175) got to the heart of it: "Privacy is minimal where technology and social organization are minimal." Furthermore, the philosophical attitude of a society plays a decisive role. "Concern for privacy tends to be high in societies espousing liberal ideals" (Bygrave 2010: 175). Moreover, more and more countries have Europeanized legislative data protection regimes, albeit their cultural concerns about privacy were actually limited (Bygrave 2010: 183).

25 In reference to the state constitutional laws, the constitutions of some states (Alaska, California, and Florida) imply an explicit right to privacy (Solove & Schwartz 2009: 34).

ment. The interpretation of privacy in the USA is strongly connected to the sphere of the house. Hence, for everything that is not bound to the home directly, a *reasonable expectation of privacy* has to exist. According to the legal interpretation of this right by the Supreme Court, to determine if a government action violates the right to privacy that is established by the Fourth Amendment, it has to be considered if the individual objectively had a reasonable expectation that these things were going to stay private (Kerr 2001: 507ff.).

This approach is also observable when looking at the US data protection regime. Contrary to the European civil rights approach of data protection, the US strategy is market-driven. This leads to a legal approach of data protection, which is sector-based instead of comprehensive data protection legislation.[26]

As far as the private sector is concerned, the US prefers a legislation that concentrates on the data holder and the type of data. It is not unusual that the same personal information is governed by two different privacy regimes depending on what kind of data holder holds the information. For instance, the holding of medical information is liable to one set of rules if the holder is a *covered entity* under the *Health Information Portability and Accountability Act*, and to another set of rules if the holder is a school (which is ruled by the *Family Educational Rights and Privacy Act*). If individuals want to protect their personal data, they need to be careful to what kind of holder the data is presented.

> While in the European Union citizens and consumers have a degree of control over how data controllers manage discrete aspects of their identities, in the […] [US] model individuals would have a (rather limited) degree of choice over *which* […] [identity provider] manages their information, but not over *how* such information is managed. […] [From an US point of view,] it seems that users would […] have the choice of which third-party identity contractor controls their personal data, rather than the enforceable rights granted to citizens of the European Union. (Holt & Malcic 2015: 165ff.)

26 One of the latest discussions about the different interpretations of privacy by Americans and Germans has been conducted by Miller (2017).

Other laws govern only certain types of data, e.g., the *Video Privacy Protection Act,* which only applies to data that are recorded on video-cassette tapes (Schwartz 2013: 1974 f.). Furthermore, the USA does not prohibit data processing unless it is specifically illegalized. Contrary, the EU forbids the use of data without a legal basis. This legal basis contains eight principles, which have to be satisfied by every data holder (approach of omnibus law instead of sectoral approach), no matter wether they are private or public:

> (1) limits on data collection, also termed data minimization; (2) the data quality principle; and (3) notice, access, and correction rights for the individual; [...] (4) a processing of personal data made only pursuant to a legal basis; (5) regulatory oversight by an independent data protection authority; (6) enforcement mechanisms, including restrictions on data exports to countries that lack sufficient privacy protection; (7) limits on automated decisionmaking; and (8) additional protection for sensitive data. (Schwartz 2013: 1976)

In the USA, data protection is subjected to just two general principles, which can be found in many legislative acts: first, the concept of notice of data processing practices and, second, the consent to this procession by the affected party. These differences exist due to the fact that data protection is – from the European point of view – part of the requirements to guarantee active citizen participation in a democratic state whereas the USA does not hold this perspective. Furthermore, the USA does not forbid the export of personal information to countries without a certain degree of data protection. In addition to that, there is no federal data protection agency. Suitable to a market-driven approach, the *Federal Trade Commission* (FTC) is responsible for the oversight. The main tasks of this authority are consumer protection and the establishment of fair practices in business, but the FTC is also responsible for privacy protection. However, there are considerable doubts as to whether the FTC can satisfy these requirements. One main point of criticism is that the FTC has – with regard to data protection – no jurisdiction over all companies and that the financial means of the FTC are not sufficient to guarantee comprehensive data protection (Schwartz 2013: 1974ff.; Bygrave 2010: 172).

Nevertheless, there exists one legislative act that deals with privacy issues in general: the *Privacy Act*. It was adopted in 1974 and prohibits the disclosure of private and medical information held by federal agencies.[27] Furthermore, it gives individuals the right of access to this information and the possibility to challenge these records. Only federal agencies have to comply with these rules and they are not applicable to private actors. Contrary to the EU approach, in the USA there exists no omnibus legislation regarding privacy (Stratford & Stradford 1998: 17ff.).

All in all, the USA prefers a model based on market conditions instead of an omnibus legislation with comprehensive data protection. However, the rest of the world follows the EU approach (Schwartz 2013: 1979). Well over 40 countries have already adopted data protection laws matching the European standard, and this number is increasing steadily (Bygrave 2010: 188).

This evolution leads to the conclusion that the norm of privacy spread through the process of digitalization because of the development of data protection.[28] Especially because of the EU's effort, data protection – and with it the protection of the private sphere – has become an issue in international relations. Nevertheless, cultural differences are still in place and have to be considered when considering the violations of the norm of privacy in the following chapter.

This chapter has shown that privacy can be considered as a fundamental human right. A comprehensive advocacy network is in place to uphold this norm. Nevertheless, it is not a *typical* one. Privacy is a dynamic and weak human rights norm: What is considered to be private changes over time and is dependent on the cultural as well as the situational context. Additionally, privacy rights can be reduced in cases of emergency. Hence, the definition Nissenbaum (2010: 231 f.) mentioned at the outset of this chapter is the most exact definition of privacy. This means that if we want to study how the norm of privacy is

27 The adoption of the Privacy Act was the result of a decade of intensive discussion. The starting point was a proposal by the Social Science Research Center to create a central government database in which all personal information about the citizens, which are held by different government authorities, could be brought together (Nissenbaum 2010: 93).

28 Even US intelligence services are included in this development. At least in theory, they agree to the norms of privacy and data protection, although their business often collides with these norms (Buckley 2014: 95ff., 101ff.).

challenged by another norm and if the norm of privacy is expiring, we always have to consider what is covered by the norm of privacy in a given context. Nevertheless, there exists one core principal of all approaches to privacy: the self-determined decision about the access to the self, particularly to the (digital and analog) flow of personal information. As a next step, the regress of this norm should be considered.

4. Norm Regression: Surveillance and Privacy in US History

Like other human rights, the norm of privacy has also been in conflict with counterterrorism measures in recent time (Heller et al. 2012: 278 f.). The NSA surveillance activities that were disclosed by Edward Snowden have been seen as the endpoint of this process for the moment. As it was argued with regard to the prohibition of torture (McKeown 2009), it is logical to assume that a norm regression has taken place. This chapter aims to explain how this development has occurred. It will explore whether the spiral model can help to explain this norm regression. This should be done in a case study focusing on US behavior with regard to mass surveillance procedures and privacy concerns.

4.1. Surveillance, Security and Privacy

Ironically, surveillance is something that is said to be as old as the human need for privacy. As a human practice, the concept of surveillance is already inherent in a mother's practice of looking after her child. It is an intrinsic feature of the human nature to care for each other. This is why surveillance is claimed to be natural. This need of care automatically results in monitoring the behavior of others. The surveillance of others, therefore, is a normal process in social settings. The aim of these monitoring processes is to nullify unaccepted behavior of members of a social group (e.g., a family or a religious group). Especially within religious beliefs, concepts of surveillance are embedded eminently. The image of an omniscient and all-seeing God helps to ensure rule consistent behavior (Goos et. al. 2015: 51 f.). "The concept of care and protectionism also transcends to the level of the state when it assumes the role of watching or surveilling its population, supposedly for its own good. This can take the form of surveillance for safety and national security" (Goos et al. 2015: 52).

State-led surveillance is not only a direct response to contemporary terror threats. In fact, surveillance was inherent to the development of the modern state. Since states have begun to raise taxes, personal information was needed. Due to this, officials started to inaugurate censuses and to establish house numbers (and faced enormous headwind by many people who were concerned about their privacy at that time). At the time of political absolutism, monarchs already decided to establish identity cards to control inhabitants in specific situations. Beside the necessity of this information for tax collection, surveillance was always justified with improving public security, in our days called *national security* (Schmale & Tinnefeld 2014: 55ff.). This is expressed in the evolution of the police in France and Britain as well as the invention of biometrics and the fingerprinting and photographing of offenders in the 19th century (Diffie & Landau 2007: 128; Agamben 2015: 7). An increase in administering public services and the creation of welfare states led to a rising demand for personal information. This is why today some scholars describe the modern bureaucracy as *infocracy* (Goos et al. 2015: 54). Indeed, this process of increased public administration normalized surveillance to some extent, "whereby citizens are being increasingly and routinely required or encouraged to provide information in exchange for access to services" (Goos et al. 2015: 54).

The establishment of electronic surveillance encouraged the increase of bureaucratic structures. It was at the end of the 19th century when the first tabulating machines were invented. These machines were necessary because of a dramatic increase of data sets during the censuses: The count of the 1880 s census in the USA took more than seven years. Thanks to the first tabulating machines this interval could be reduced to three years during the 1890 s US census. Until the 1960 s, electronic-mechanic tabulating machines and punch cards remained the primary way of information processing and were used by government agencies and companies. But the invention of the first computer in the 1940 s challenged this process. In 1951, the US Bureau of the Census acquired the first commercially marketed computer. This development – in addition to the emergence of databases – made it easier and faster to analyze data for the purpose of surveillance (Goos et al. 2015: 55).

The 1960 s and 1970 s can be considered as a time of general crisis. From the end of colonialism via the Cold War and Vietnam War to the beginning of the end of Fordist capitalism and the new threat through communism regimes, these developments were responded to by terms of surveillance. Specifically, the eagerness of the USA and the Soviet Union to participate in the Cold War led to the invention of powerful technologies to collect, store and process data. Hence, criminal records and other state-led databases emerged (Goos et al. 2015: 55ff.). And also "[i]ntelligence services augmented their capacities to monitor citizens through the use of information technology for the surveillance systems applied for national security" (Goos et al. 2015: 57). After the 9/11 terror attacks, surveillance practices increased. Although surveillance had been increasingly accepted as a part of everyday life before 2001 (since the 1990 s the term *surveillance society* took shape in public discussion (Lyon 2015: 28)), heretofore it has become more obvious (Goos et al. 2015: 71 f.).

Surveillance merely describes the process of information collection in order to manage control (Lyon 2015: 3). Surveillance, thereby, creates a power structure between the controller and the surveilled person. This power structure is always in support of the controller. This phenomenon is of increasing importance in an information society, because more and more data emerge. But the bare process of informatization of society and the collection of emerging data is not what challenges the norm of privacy. It is the normative argument that is brought forward to implement surveillance (Zurawski 2015: 14 f.).

First and foremost, security and surveillance are two different things. Security is an even broader term than privacy. Only that much is clear: Security describes a condition. What kind of condition that can be, is dependent on the context. Hence, and unsurprisingly, security can be connected to plenty of areas and can be defined in multiple ways. By talking of security in this and the following chapters, a conception of security is meant that consists in the protection of a state's population and infrastructure. This is the same understanding of security that is held by security agencies (Zurawski 2015: 20).

The connection of both security and surveillance resides in the usage of security as a rhetoric device to describe a condition that can only be achieved with surveillance measures. Hence, security can justify the implementation of surveillance measures (Zurawski 2015: 22). By the argumentative use of the term security, it can create a norm itself. The following case study explores the influence of the norm of security to the regress of the norm of privacy. While having taken a look at the concept of the norm of privacy, we also need to briefly consider the conception of the security norm as well as the contrast to the privacy norm.

As mentioned above, given the rise of the Cold War and the emerging intelligence capabilities of states, surveillance practices are increasingly justified with *national security*. The term was shaped by the National Security Act of 1947, which, among other things, created the Central Intelligence Agency (CIA). Albeit the term was the name of a legal act, the term was never defined (Theoharis 2011: 35 f.).[29]

With the term of national security, the norm of security was constructed in a way that challenges the norm of privacy progressively. Not only because the security norm had broadened since the 1950s

29 One of the most exact attempts to confine this term can be found in the 1950s when efforts failed to legalize wiretapping in Congress. Accordingly, national security was delineated as acts encompassing "treason, sabotage, espionage, sedition, sedition conspiracy, violation of the neutrality laws, violation of the Act requiring the registration of agents of foreign principals, … violation of the Act requiring the registration of organizations carrying on certain activities within the United States … [and] violation of the Atomic Energy Act of 1946" (US House 1953, cited in Theoharis 2011: 35 f.).
Although the term *national security* was never defined, government officials tried from the 1950s on to introduce that term into the debate. With the upcoming and ever more escalating Cold War, state officials wanted to ensure that sufficient juridical leeway existed to ensure the permissiveness of bugging and wiretapping practices. Hence, they started to "theorize about a 'national security' exception to the Fourth Amendment" (Atkinson 2015: 11). As an example, Herbert Brownell, Eisenhower's Attorney General, held that "in some instances the use of microphone surveillance is the only possible way of uncovering the activities of espionage agents, possible saboteurs, and subversive persons [thus] the national interest requires that microphone surveillance be utilized by the Federal Bureau of Investigation" (Brownell 1954, cited in Atkinson 2015: 11).

(Daase & Rühlig 2016: 13 f.; Katzenstein 1996: 10 f.) privacy was encountered, but also because this security norm is by definition a contradiction to the norm of privacy. The theoretical foundation of the security norm is the Hobbesian thinking of a state. People have to give up their freedom to gain security. Their unification creates the all-seeing Leviathan with God-like attributes protecting the people from the state of nature. The threat of the *bellum omnium contra omnes* makes the people create a state as a protection device (Schweidler 2014: 93; Hempel et al. 2011: 7).

This thinking drives the justification of surveillance, which also challenges the existing rule of law in liberal states (Opitz & Tellmann 2011). To govern, that means to ensure the security of people, visibility is necessary. Monitoring is inevitable for the Leviathan to exercise power, to create security. This kind of thinking counters the norm of privacy fundamentally, because privacy rests on the idea of Kantian autonomy. Privacy means the possibility of invisibility! The individually determined distribution of visibility is the expression of a liberal state conception with emancipated individuals. Thus, according to Warren and Brandeis, privacy means freedom, a freedom that is guaranteed by the absence of state interventions, by the right to be let alone. The ideal of the privacy norm is to secure people from the state (Haas 2014: 29 f.; Hempel et al. 2011: 12 f.).[30]

The development of globalization as well as the consequently emerging *risk society*, a term shaped by Ulrich Beck (1986), enhanced the security norm immensely. The emergence of a pre-crime society is the result of the will to avoid risks of the future. As a result of the ideal of precaution, more and more data are collected and shared internationally with the aim to foresee future risks; the collection activities of the NSA and the sharing of information with other agencies, disclosed by Snowden, are examples. Although there is no reliable evidence that the underlying assumption – more data, better prevention – is true, the alleged effectiveness of surveillance measures is an important argument in the public debate in favor of enhanced surveillance authorities

30 This does not mean that the norm of privacy is in general incompatible with the Hobbesian state conception. Indeed, in a liberal state conception individuals rely also on state interventions, but interventions that secure their privacy (Hempel et al. 2011: 12).

of the state (Hegemann & Kahl 2016). This makes sense with regard to the Hobbesian theory, which is first and foremost a state concept of enlightenment and rationality (Hempel et al. 2011: 7). Hobbes created one of the first state theories that does not rely on transcendental arguments; the creation of the Leviathan is driven by the rational choice of the people. Hence, the justification of measures to create visibility has to rely on rational arguments.

Krasmann (2011) has shown that these developments do not necessarily end in the classical conception of a repressive surveillance state. Instead, security measures including the collection of personal data without probable cause are increasingly accepted. This is considered to be a change of the norm: Non-action is seen as too risky, permanent collection and the enduring search for risks are considered to be logical (Hegemann & Kahl 2016: 202). NSA chief Keith Alexander gave an example of this point of view when he expressed that, instead of finding the needle in the haystack, "let's collect the whole haystack. Collect it all, tag it, store it… And whatever it is you want, you go searching for it" (cited in Nakashima & Warrick 2013).

The implementation of new surveillance tools is often justified in reference to an impending threat and the resulting necessity. Privacy concerns are often swept aside by putting security and liberty (or privacy, respectively) in the metaphor of a balance and by arguing that the necessity outweighed privacy, especially in cases of counterterrorism policy. Although the struggle for the correct balance between these two values is often conceived as age-old, President Truman made the first reference in 1951 when he designated Admiral Nimitz to head a presidential commission on secrecy by asking him to "seek the wisest balance that can be struck between security and freedom" (cited in Cullather 2015: 21). Such a commission was necessary after government programs had been revealed with the aim to secure the loyalty of civil servants in the McCarthy era and during the war against Communism (Cullather 2015: 21 f.) Although this metaphor suggests that both security and privacy interests should equally be acknowledged, this is not as obvious as it seems. Indeed, this metaphor is problematic because it takes security and liberty as a zero sum game. Thereby, it follows the Hobbesian roots, whereupon 100 percent security is only possible by giving up 100 percent of one's liberty. And the maximum amount of liberty is only possible without any security. Furthermore, in practice this balance mostly contains the security interests of the majority and the civil liberties of a few, which results in tipping the balance in favor of security. Additionally, whereas liberty is a present interest, security is a norm bound to future uncertainties. From the standpoint of the security norm, it is always more favorable to avoid future uncertainties instead of keeping present interests (Zedner 2009: 135ff.).

The balance metaphor is one main argumentative figure to encounter human rights norms. It aims to redefine the scope of a norm and to justify its violation or non-applicability. Especially in the following two chapters, this kind of argumentation is of importance.

Surveillance[31] is the collection of information in order to manage control (Lyon 2015: 3). For the purpose of this paper, surveillance is defined as the routine control of human beings or their devices with the intention to protect, understand, ensure entitlement, control or influence groups or individuals (Lyon 2015: 3). This kind of surveillance can be done in two ways: personal surveillance and mass surveillance. Clarke (1988) defines both as follows:

> Personal surveillance is the surveillance of an identified person. In general, a specific reason exists for the investigation or monitoring. Mass surveillance is the surveillance of groups of people, usually large groups. In general, the reason for investigation or monitoring is to identify indi-

31 Contrary to the field of privacy, the concept of surveillance is highly *undertheorized*. The main concept to theorize surveillance has been the panopticism Michel Foucault invented in the 1970 s. His work was crucial to initiate the emergence of surveillance studies (Lyon et. al. 2014: 4 f.). Unfortunately, scholars have lacked to emancipate and failed to develop new convincing approaches to theorize surveillance. The first scholars that criticized the supremacy of the panopticon model were Haggerty and Ericson (2000). They questioned if this concept was still useful to understand modern surveillance in all possible aspects. It is also queried by economics, as they see multiple aspects of surveillance conducted by more than one actor as well as individuals shifting between being the controller and being controlled (Brivot & Gendron 2011). Horowitz (2017) voiced similar criticism. That is why some scholars avoid the term *surveillance*. Instead, they use new terms like *monitoring* and *tracking*. This should avoid the automatic conjecture that surveillance was performed from *above*, "as subjects of surveillance are monitored by those in authority or more powerful than them" (Nissenbaum 2010: 22).

> viduals who belong to some particular class of interest to the surveillance organization. (Clarke 1988: 499)

Personal surveillance does not contradict the norm of privacy generally, because it is targeted. Especially in modern democracies, the need for law enforcement and the human right to privacy are balanced: A court warrant is needed for the intrusion of the private sphere of an individual. Mass surveillance, also called dragnet surveillance, is not possible without violating the norm of privacy in general. This is why I am going to concentrate on the development of mass surveillance in this chapter.

It is beyond the scope of this paper to consider every possible kind of mass surveillance. This is why one special approach should be considered. "One of the classical approaches to surveillance is the eavesdropping of communication and interaction between citizens, originally over the telephone network, but more recently also over the Internet" (Goos et al. 2015: 57). In this chapter, I will concentrate on this approach of surveillance, because it is specific enough to guarantee efficient research, and it was conducted over a long period in history, which guarantees an insight into the development of mass surveillance and privacy. Other, newer forms of mass surveillance, like the surveillance of public places by cameras (CCTV) or surveillance measures at airports, will not be considered in order to reduce the scope of mass surveillance measures I am going to talk about.

This approach is also in line with the definition of privacy in the previous chapter. According to rulings by the Supreme Court (in 1937), there exists a reasonable expectation of privacy regarding the content of phone calls. Also, the collection of metadata is considered to be a breach of the norm of privacy. Although the Supreme Court had ruled as recently as 2010 and 2015[32] about the unlawfulness of metadata collection, this judgment was anticipated by state officials as soon as the metadata collection came up in the 1990 s, as I will show below.

Since this chapter explores the surveillance of communications and interactions of citizens conducted by a state, this chapter will mainly focus on the policy of intelligence activities, because most often

32 United States v. Warshak as well as ACLU v. Clapper are the respective court rulings.

they are the state organizations that are best skilled to conduct mass surveillance. This chiefly includes two areas of intelligence: communications intelligence (COMINT) and signals intelligence (SIGINT).[33]

Hence, in this case study we will explore the policy of mass surveillance conducted by the USA – mainly by the Federal Bureau of Investigations (FBI), the CIA and the NSA – through the use of COMINT and SIGINT, that aim to monitor the communications and interactions of US citizens as well as, in the last part of the chapter, foreigners. I will not only concentrate on the activities of intelligence agencies but also on the normative justification of these procedures by politicians and officials as well as on the legislation regarding surveillance practices by intelligence agencies.

The focus on domestic surveillance is necessary, because general surveillance practices are commonly conducted by states.[34] Since the emergence of the first multiethnic states, state leaders have made their officials engage in surveillance in order to learn the attitudes and plans

33 COMINT, defined as extracting information from communications, is the oldest way of state agencies to intercept one's privacy. The steady migration of communication from older, less accessible medias to new and more accessible ways of communicating has made signals intelligence (SIGINT, which means "the information obtained by analyzing signals emitted by a target" (Diffie & Landau 2007: 93)) very important to COMINT. The huge accessibility of communications in these days makes experts speaking of "a golden age" of COMINT (Diffie & Landau 2007: 104). This unfortunately very often leads to a confusion of SIGINT and COMINT or to the constellation that one might think SIGINT was another term for COMINT. But this is wrong, since there are other areas of SIGINT that are not related to COMINT, e.g. radar intelligence, telemetry intelligence and emissions intelligence. Hence, COMINT is just one aspect of SIGINT. Besides that, the main target of COMINT is the acquisition of signals in any form (paper, radio waves, electrical currents in wires, disks, tapes etc.), thus, COMINT can also be conducted without using SIGINT (Diffie & Landau 2007: 88ff.).

34 A picturesque example, which makes this point very clear, is the conference in 1945 where the UN was founded. At the same time as the delegates of the world's nations debated in San Francisco about the foundation of the organization that should later be an advocate to the right to privacy, the USA spied on every delegation and read the telegraphs they sent to their headquarters at home. It is also no coincidence that the UN headquarter is placed in New York. Among other reasons, the USA wanted to encourage and simplify the work of their agents that are engaged in surveillance activities (Hager 2015: 10).

of opponent states.[35] Hence, there has never been a right to privacy for states. Also international law does not prohibit intelligence activities. As there is a difference between domestic and foreign surveillance, it is not surprising that in many countries two different agencies are concerned with these two practices (e.g., the MI5 and MI6 or the FBI and CIA/NSA). The Snowden revelations have caused a discussion about the validity of this fragmentation. I will address this topic at the end of this chapter; nevertheless this is a very new development. In order to reach a comparability with older forms of mass surveillance, one must first focus on mass surveillance of US citizens, because, as Mills (2015: 196) put it: "Domestic surveillance creates an inevitable collision of two legal principles and basic human instincts – security and privacy." Thus, to find out if the norm of privacy is still in place it makes sense to look at the domestic level of surveillance.

4.2. From Roosevelt to the Church Committee

As surveillance is an omnipresent part in and of humanity and in the history of mankind, it is unsurprising that the story of US mass surveillance starts at the very beginning of US history. When the Founding Fathers of the US created the Fourth Amendment that protects citizens against unreasonable searches and seizures, a grievance against the behavior of the British occupiers was expressed. British soldiers and officials commonly conducted general searches. The hostility against occupiers going door-to-door and person-to-person was huge;

35 There is one famous exception to this rule in history: Shortly after Henry Stimson was appointed US Secretary of State in 1929, officials told him about Japanese communication that had been intercepted and deciphered by the Cipher Bureau, informally known as the *Black Chamber* and a predecessor of the NSA. His reaction to this was harsh. He judged that this behavior was "highly unethical" and concluded with a statement that should become famous: "Gentlemen do not read each other´s mail" (cited in Chesterman 2011: 1). It should stay a rare glimpse of the norm of privacy in international state-to-state relations. As a consequence, the *Black Chamber's* budget was reduced and finally closed (Chesterman 2011: 1).

the corollary was the adoption of the Fourth Amendment (Cate 2015: 39).[36]

However, this did not prevent officials of the USA to try and break this rule. The first case of mass surveillance in US history can be found during the Civil War in the 1860 s. Abraham Lincoln founded the first intelligence-collection agency in the USA, headed by Allan Pinkerton who was highly interested in a new invention: the telegraph. With the beginning of the Civil War, the government sought to gain control over the wires. In addition to that, they seized copies of all telegrams that had been sent in the last twelve months (companies held these copies for reasons of account keeping). After the war the US government continued to ask for copies of all telegrams that were sent. This caused a privacy advocacy process to be led by the telegraph companies, which wanted to assure their costumers that their communications would be private. The companies claimed that the same legal protection should be provided to telegrams as to US mail. Because the government neglected these claims, the telegram providers went to court. In 1879, the Missouri Supreme Court did not follow the approach of the telegram companies, but it ruled that request for telegram copies would have to specify the date and the subject of the message and thus prohibited a mass surveillance approach (Atkinson 2015: 8; Diffie & Landau 2007: 146 f.).

As a matter of course, this case cannot be fully analyzed with the spiral model. First, the right to privacy was not yet invented – albeit it was already in the air – and although the government tried to get access to all telegrams, telegraphs were not widespread; not every individual had its own telegraph. Nevertheless, already in this early case, after the first technical invention that made communication more accessible, one can observe a government that is not acting on behalf of the privacy norm (here: privacy as a social norm, not as a human right), and actors who activate and the advocacy process that led in the

36 Whereas the norm of privacy is reflected in the Fourth Amendment without mentioning the word *privacy* in particular the norm of security – often used to justify surveillance – is included in phrases like "provide for the common defense" or "secure the Blessings of Liberty to ourselves and our Posterity" (Mills 2015: 196).

very end to the limitation of governance actions, ensuring that government actions were set straight.

The second case in US history where US officials conducted mass surveillance was brought to light one century later, in the 1970 s. The surveillance of suspected communists, civil rights activists and journalists had its roots in the 1930 s. With the evolvement of new technical opportunities and the development of modern, technology-based intelligence agencies in the early 20th century,[37] the opportunities for the violation of the right to privacy grew, as I will explore in the following.[38]

Ironically, none other than President Franklin Roosevelt, one of the main supporters of the idea of universal human rights, authorized wiretapping activities, which were done by the FBI, for the first time. These wiretaps could be conducted by secret orders form presidents, Attorney Generals or the FBI director. With this authorization, the focus of FBI work shifted from pure law enforcement to monitoring *subversives*. This happened in 1934, the very same year in which Congress banned wiretapping in general by adopting the Communications Act, the first legal framework for such operations. FBI officials claimed that

37 Most Western intelligence agencies have their roots in the early years of the 20th century. The reason for the establishment of such agencies was an increasing fear of spies. In the USA as well as in Europe countries feared not only that in case of war foreigners or people with foreign ancestors could hand on national secrets but also that they could act as a *fifth column*, always ready to support their home countries. In the USA, at the beginning of the century a need for federal capacities of criminal investigation was identified, and Attorney General Bonaparte founded an unnamed investigative bureau in 1908, which was named the *Bureau of Investigations* one year later. Because of domestic bombing attacks as well as the increasing fear of spies during World War I, the *General Intelligence Division* was founded within the Bureau of Investigations, headed by the young and ambitioned commander J. Edgar Hoover (Boghosian 2013: 71 f.).

38 The first years of domestic surveillance activities in the USA are the ones that have not been broadly studied yet. Due to the absence of a broad research literature, the first part of the following chapter is mainly based on the work of Athan Theoharis (2011), which is one of the first comprehensive works on this field (together with Greenberg (2010)). Before, monographs were only covering special events of surveillance, like the surveillance of the Martin Luther King movement or Hollywood stars.

this prohibition was not valid for federal agents and that it only needed to be respected by private individuals and corporations. This is why Justice Department officials continued to authorize wiretaps during criminal investigations. But the Supreme Court disagreed and ruled in 1937 that the ban of wiretapping also applied to FBI agents. Nonetheless, FBI director J. Edgar Hoover instructed his agents to continue the wiretapping. But after a second Supreme Court ruling against this practice, Hoover had reservations about continuing this performance and stopped illegal wiretapping. As a consequence, he informally pushed for new legislations maintaining that certain FBI investigations are impossible under this law, e.g., the prevention of kidnapping, espionage and national catastrophes (Atkinson 2015: 8; Theoharis 2011: 24ff.).

As one can see, denial and justification were used to circumvent the norm of privacy. At this point, we can observe the first activation of the spiral model. The government allowed an intrusion into the private sphere without a court order. Hence, the USA declined from step five the rule-consistent behavior to step four the prescriptive status where the domestic laws are still adjusted to the norm of privacy. Also the mainstream discourse upholds the norm of privacy; otherwise the actors (in this case, the President as well as the FBI director) would not fear to make their actions and supporting arguments public. But they did. This shows that the validity of the right to privacy is still accepted in general, although actors try to challenge this norm by creating a competing security norm. It is maintained that this new norm is more valuable than the existing norm and that new laws should be created to establish this new norm (new laws allowing the surveillance of possible spies). Nevertheless, when the misconduct became public, an advocacy network set in – in this case, the advocate was a plaintive one and a court, not a NGO – to punish the misbehavior, because the arguments advocating the encountering norm (security) are not valued higher by the court. Therefore, the USA rose from step four to step five again.

However, the next decline was not long in the coming: President Roosevelt shared Hoover's view in parts and secretly authorized FBI wiretappings again in May 1940. Roosevelt was especially worried about potential German and Soviet spies in the USA. He circumvented the Supreme Court ruling with the argument that the court never made a dictum that applied "to grave matters involving the defense of the nation" (Roosevelt 1940, cited in Theoharis 2011: 27). Roosevelt tried to build up a challenging narrative: A special area, one of national interest, exists in which the existing privacy norm cannot be applied. This moment can also be considered to be the trigger to enhance a normative dynamic that created a norm that should later be connected with the word national security. The window of opportunity for the creation of this norm was World War II.

With this argumentation, Roosevelt authorized wiretaps "on the prior review and approval, on a case-by-case basis, of the attorney general" (Theoharis 2011: 27) and only in cases that are "confined to investigations 'of persons suspected of subversive activities against the United States, including suspected spies' and were to be 'conducted to a minimum and to limit them insofar as possible to aliens'" (Theoharis 2011: 27).

According to Attorney General Jackson, this was against the law, and he was afraid of a public debate in the case of discovery. In other words: He was aware of the existing privacy norm. Thus, Jackson decided that Hoover should not provide a detailed record of the secret wiretaps. Thereby, he wanted to reduce the risk of discovery. Roosevelt's requirements for wiretapping were hereby subverted. Future Attorney Generals could only learn about existing secret wiretaps through the FBI director. In addition to that, Jackson did not demand reauthorizations of existing wiretaps. Hence, FBI agents were not required to explain after a certain amount of time if the originally stated security threat was still existent. This *modus operandi* was in place until the 1970s when Attorney General Edward Levi discovered these practices inadvertently (Theoharis 2011: 27).

One has to give credit to Jackson that he did not plan to uphold this procedure for an indefinite amount of time. Instead, he asked Congress in 1940 for a change to the law so wiretaps would be legal in cases of espionage. But his bid failed, and Congress did not approve of the bill proposed by Congressman Celler notably because liberals doubted that wiretaps would be confined to legitimate security threats and assumed that the government would use such a law to spy on political activists and ordinary people (Theoharis 2011: 29 f.).

The Pearl Harbor attacks in December 1941 and the following US involvement in World War II made Celler again propose a bill for the legalization of wiretapping. Expecting headwind in Congress, Celler's proposal limited wiretapping to the duration of the war and to counterespionage activities. But his attempt failed again. Nonetheless, the FBI continued wiretapping, based solely on Roosevelts secret directive, maintaining that these procedures were necessary in times of war. However, during the war the FBI engaged in wiretapping activities that had not been covered by the Roosevelt doctrine: Political activists of labor union and civil-rights movements were under scrutiny, and the FBI conducted spying on them; these mass surveillance practices were later conducted under the name Counter Intelligence Program (COINTELPRO). After World War II was ended, Hoover pushed for the authorization of these measures by President Truman. The president's broader conception of national security threats as well as the upcoming Cold War made this attempt successful. In a letter to Truman, Hoover asked for an extension of wiretaps to cases "virtually affecting the domestic security, or where human life is in jeopardy" (Hoover 1946, cited in Theoharis 2011: 31). In addition to that, he skipped Roosevelts sentence that required such practices to be conducted at a minimum level. By signing this letter, Truman unleashed the FBI's wiretapping measures. Nevertheless, the FBI actions were authorized but not legalized (Theoharis 2011: 30 f.). Because it was again a secret order that allowed wiretapping, the actors were aware of the existing norm of privacy.

In addition to this, after World War II, the USA started the intelligence operation SHAMROCK. During the war, the American telegraph companies *ITT World Communications*, *Western Union International* and *RCA Global* had transmitted all incoming and outgoing telegraphs to military intelligence. This was legal under wartime legislation. But military intelligence officials wanted to keep this procedure going after the end of the war. Hence, they established SHAMROCK in August 1945, and persuaded the chiefs of the telegram companies that this procedure was legal (Theoharis 2011: 162 f.). This was necessary because the norm of privacy was still in place. Whereas Western Union just handed over the telegrams of and to intelligence targets, both the ITT and RCA provided the full bulk of all telegrams they received. Analysts of the Armed Forces Security Agency (AFSA; the predecessor of the NSA) read the communications of foreigners and Americans who were placed on a watch list (Diffie & Landau 2007: 158).

It took until 1949, until surveillance hit the public debate: Judith Coplon was arrested and accused. The Russian spy Coplon was detained while meeting a Russian agent to deliver 28 secret FBI reports. During the proceedings the reports were submitted to her attorney to face the charge. Hence, the 28 reports came to light in public and it turned out that not one of it revealed national secrets. Instead, it became apparent that the FBI investigated American political activists and that the information that were obtained from wiretaps. Public furor was the result of the seeming confirmation of extensive FBI wiretapping activities and it forced the Justice Department to publish a statement in March 1949, which stated that wiretaps were only conducted "in limited cases with the express approval in each instance of the Attorney General. There has been no new policy or procedure since the initial policy was stated by President Roosevelt and this has continued to be the Department's policy when the security of the nation is involved" (cited in Theoharis 2011: 32). Hereinafter, the White House staff scrutinized these cases and came to the result that the Hoover letter signed by Truman dropped any boundary to wiretaps (Theoharis 2011: 32 f.).

Truman responded immediately and drafted a new wiretapping authority that restricted wiretapping to "cases where the national security requires it" (cited in Theoharis 2011: 33); furthermore, the Attorney General should be asked to assure control of these measures. But this conviction was short-lived. President Truman never executed this directive because of the high anti-Communist climate of that time, often framed as *McCarthyism*[39]. The White House came to the conclusion that it would be too costly to reduce the FBI's wiretapping authority. Instead, they pushed Congress to legalize wiretaps to the prior approval of the Attorney General, but these attempts failed again (Theoharis 2011: 33).

Here the spiral model fails to explain the developments. According to the model, an advocacy process should have set in after the Coplon case, but this did not happen. The political climate at that time blocked this process. Instead, in this climate it was of high value to spread the norm of security to other state actors.

Hereinafter, the Justice Department also internalized the security norm. According to the Attorney General, every discussion in Congress about legalizing wiretaps could lead to the unwanted result that eavesdropping is only allowed on grounds of a court warrant. In fact, this was the controversial point for an entire decade in which President Eisenhower came to power. Five times in the 1950 s – in 1953, 1954, 1955, 1958, and 1959 – Congress debated about legalizing

39 McCarthyism was defined by President Truman in 1953 (cited in Doherty 2003: 15) as "the rise to power of the demagogue who lives on untruth; it is the spread of fear and the destruction of faith in every level of our society." The word goes back to the Republican Senator Joseph R. McCarthy. Until today his name symbolizes the "demonic zeitgeist, a shorthand term for the stifling of free debate and the denial of constitutional rights by the imputation of communist sympathies" (Doherty 2003:14). This anti-communist zeitgeist was predated and postdated to McCarthy's public appearance in the 1950 s. The first roots of it can be found in the 1920 s and it lasted until the end of the Cold War (Schrecker 2002: 12ff.). After World War II McCarthyism was also linked to the development of the *national security* term that transformed communism to a threat the nation is facing (Schrecker 2002: 20ff.; Schrecker 1998: 86ff.).
Originally, McCarthy was a first-string player for only four years, beginning with a speech in February 1950 claiming that he possessed a list of 205 known communists in the State Department (what proved to be a lie). From this moment on, he was one of the country's best known anti-communist politicians who fanned fear of Communists undermining the country. His tactic of *Red-baiting* was also used to confront labor unions "without having to address economic issues" (Schrecker 2002: 13). His demagogic tactics were dismantled by a TV report in 1954 – one of the first dismantlings in TV history (Doherty 2003: 14 f.).
Today, the term *McCarthyism* is used to describe in general a policy of false accusation and suspicions without any proof (Schrecker 2002: 1ff.).

eavesdropping. Unlike the White House, the Justice Department and the FBI preferred to allow eavesdropping under the sole supervision of the Attorney General. But Congress denied authorizing these drafts. On the contrary, some Congressmen wanted wiretaps to be established by court warrants so that the privacy norm would be still unimpaired, but FBI officials heavily opposed this solution and they lobbied Congress to prevent such a result. A big discussion was held about the question of what should be defined as national security (Theoharis 2011: 34 f.). At the same time, in 1952, Truman founded the NSA, which would later become "the largest, most expensive, and most technologically advanced spy organization on the planet" (Bamford 2009: 13).[40]

---

40 The founding of the NSA was the result of the bad condition of US SIGINT at that time. Originally, SIGINT was in the responsibility of the Army. The Signal Security Agency (SSA) was the Armys SIGINT collecting organization (the navys organization was named Naval Security Group (NSG) and also the air force had her own SIGINT organization, the Air Force Security Service (AFSS)). All its intercepted material was sent to the Special Branch, a component of Army G-2, a department founded after the Pearl Harbor attacks. Whereas the Special Branch was responsible for analyzing SIGINT materials, the rest of Army G-2 worked on other materials like military attaché reports. During World War II, the Americans aggregated considerable SIGINT capabilities.
From 1943 on, the US Armys SIGINT collections focus shifted from classical military communication to diplomatic communications because of the dramatic changes in the global geopolitical balance of power. With this shift the US wanted to *win the peace,* expecting massive advantages in future peace talks that would inevitably follow the war. After the war, the SSA was redesigned as the Army Security Agency (ASA) – but had one big problem: The war was over, and all the intelligence analysts were not needed anymore. 120 days after Japan surrendered, the army and navy lost 80 percent of their COMINT analysts, which were part of the SIGINT collection departments.
In 1949, the Armed Forces Security Agency (AFSA) was founded to combine the agencies of the army, navy and air force. But AFSA lacked money, personnel and equipment. Hence, they were totally unprepared for the Korean War that began in 1950. Because the AFSA throughout the whole war failed to gain essential intelligence insights into the Chinese/North-Korean communications, the CIA director, the minister of defense as well as the minister of foreign affairs demanded an investigation of these occurrences. The result was the *Brownell Committee Report.* This report recommended to replace the AFSA with a new unified SIGINT agency that should centralize the SIGINT effort of the US government. In October 24, 1952, Truman signed an eight-page directive, which created the NSA. The new agency

Of all these developments, the practices of the FBI remained relatively unaffected. Eisenhower won the election with a militant anti-communist stance and his Attorney General, Brownell, also reflected this point of view. In May 1954, he issued a secret directive allowing FBI officials to install wiretaps and bugs – including means of trespass. These measures of eavesdropping were authorized "in connection with matters related to internal security" (Brownell 1954, cited in Theoharis 2011: 37); in addition to that, he hold that for the FBI to "fulfill its intelligence function, considerations of internal security and the national safety are paramount and, therefore, may compel the unrestricted use of this technique in the national interest" (Brownell 1954, cited in Theoharis 2011: 38). However, also Brownell did not create detailed records of FBI eavesdropping requests and to what extend FBI officials were encouraged to carry out their spying activities. FBI agents, in some cases, did not even have to obtain permission for monitoring in advance (Theoharis 2011: 37 f.).

In the 1960 s, Congress legalized eavesdropping for the first time in history – without lobbying efforts of the Johnson administration, instead with the support of Southern Democrats and conservative Republicans. The security norm was a matter of public debate, able to diminish the effectiveness of the privacy norm. Driven by a political climate of *law and order* in the face of a growing anti-Vietnam War and civil-rights movements, Congress adopted the Omnibus Crime Control and Safe Streets Act of 1968. This bill legalized wiretapping subject to a court warrant. Nevertheless, a big exception was made: Eavesdropping activities that were conducted to enhance *national security* did not require court warrants. Nothing in this act aimed to limit these wiretapping authorities of the President. Proponents of this legislation were not convinced that this broad language could prompt the President to authorize eavesdropping measures against political activists.

was placed out of the rubric of existing intelligence agencies and was not, like all others, supervised by the CIA. Instead, the NSA was placed within the ambit of the Defense Department. The formation of this new agency happened widely unnoticed by the public – also because November 4 was Presidential Election Day: Eisenhower won against Stevenson (Aid 2009: 2–45).

Instead, John McCellan, the bill's floor manager, maintained that this bill would protect the communications privacy of Americans (Theoharis 2011: 41).

The spiral model cannot explain this development. Step three of the spiral model – called tactical concessions – would demand that the USA withdraw from international treaties that call for the right to privacy or that the USA oppose them publicly. But this did not happen. As McCellans comment showed, politicians were convinced that with the Omnibus Act of 1968 the private sphere of Americans was protected. Furthermore, it can be doubted whether the legalization of wiretapping without a warrant for national security purposes can still be classified as prescriptive status. The Omnibus Act included very big concessions to the supporters of the security norm.

The FBI used the Omnibus Act extensively. The Bureau saw the mainly peaceful protests for civil rights and against the Vietnam War, as well as riots of black people as domestic upheaval. The FBI heavily surveilled black neighborhoods after riots in Los Angeles in 1965. Up to 7,400 informants worked in the black ghettos for the FBI until the early 1970s. The same happened with the women's liberation movement and anti-Vietnam War movement. In 1970, the US Army "maintained files on at least 100,000 Americans" (Diffie & Landau 2007: 162). When Richard Nixon became President in 1969, his administration authorized political wiretapping[41] within four months. Journalists were distinctively monitored by this approach of targeted surveillance, but also political opponents were spied on, which later became known as the *Watergate scandal* (Diffie & Landau 2007: 165).

The political attitude of the Nixon White House enhanced FBI surveillance activities. Nixon was highly concerned about the increasing activities of the student Left, which committed more than 250

41 Nixon was not the first president who authorized political spying. Roosevelt issued the very first political wiretap in 1940 when he requested the wiretapping of Henry Grunewald who was officially believed to head a German espionage ring. The investigation did not prove Grunewald to be a spy. But apart from that, the wiretapping revealed useful information about the tactics of politically isolated opponents of Roosevelt, because Grunewald cultivated contacts with those people (Theoharis 2011: 46 f.).

bombings to protest against the Vietnam War. In August 1970, the FBI planned to intensify COINTELPRO, fearing extremist organizations plans to kidnap Government officials and their family members. Under the command of Nixon, the government even developed a detailed plan for domestic eavesdropping: the so-called Huston plan (Greenberg 2010: 70ff.). Nixon himself justified its development, citing security reasons, when he told the intelligence chiefs: "We are now confronted with a new and grave crisis in our country. Certainly hundreds, perhaps thousands of Americans – mostly under 30 – are determined to destroy our society" (cited in Greenberg 2010: 70).

White House staffer Tom Huston was put in charge of developing a plan to pool all intelligence resources to fight domestic unrest. This resulted in the proposal to conduct spying on dissenters directly from the White House. In his report, Huston acknowledged the existence of the privacy norm stating that "[c]onvert [mail] coverage is illegal, and there are serious risks involved," but denied to follow this norm because "the advantages to be derived from its use outweigh the risks" (Huston 1970, cited in Diffie & Landau 2007: 165). Nixon approved of this plan, but five days before it became effective he rescinded his approval. Hoover, of all people, objected to the plan because he feared public reaction in case the plan would reveal to the public; additionally, he was not open to sharing information with other state agencies (Diffie & Landau 2007: 159ff.). Nevertheless, the Huston plan can be considered to be the first well-structured plan of domestic mass surveillance activities in the USA that would have tipped the balance further in favor of the security norm. But due to concerns that a possible privacy advocacy process might be too strong, these attempts were not realized.

Over all these eavesdropping measures described above, a veil of silence was drawn. The success of avoiding public scrutiny ended in the early 1970s and, thus, activated an advocacy process. It all started with a revelation in 1970 saying that the FBI engaged in surveillance on people planning the Earth Day rally. Included in the surveillance was Senator Muskie, who was one of the speakers at that day (Christie 1972: 873). One year later, leftist activists burgled the FBI's resident bureau in Media and stole 1,000 classified documents. This was followed by the end of COINTELPRO of the FBI in spring 1971, fearing revelations. The disclosures were published one year later in several newspapers and they brought to light that the FBI was conducting surveillance on US citizens. The Freedom of Information Act suit by journalist Carl Stern resulted in the release of even more FBI reports revealing FBI's COINTELPRO. In 1972 and 1973, the Watergate scandal was brought to light: the exploitation of the resources of US intelligence agencies for political purposes – in particular, the surveillance of the Democratic Party – by the Nixon administration was uncovered. Furthermore, in December 1974 the *New York Times* published an article that exposed both the CIA's domestic surveillance program CHAOS and the CIA's attempt to undermine the government of Chile because President Allende had been too critical of the USA. Only a few months later, Attorney General Edward Levi had to confess that former FBI Director Hoover had maintained secret reports on activities of prominent Americans (Greenberg 2010: 74; Johnson 2008: 38; Theoharis 2011: 141 f.).

These mixtures of occurrences initiated an advocacy process. The public upheaval that followed these developments resulted in the *Year of Intelligence*, "the year when the question of how to manage the nation's secret agencies emerged as a key topic of debate in Washington" (Johnson 2008: 38). At the beginning of 1975, three investigative committees were created to scrutinize governmental and intelligence activities. All committees were named after their chairmen. The *Church Committee* (Senate), the *Pike Committee* (House) and the *Rockefeller Committee*[42] (White House) investigated the occurrences. Because the Church Committee remained on the investigative trail for the longest

42 The official names of the committees are *The Senate Select Committee to Study Governmental Operation with Respect to Intelligence Activities*, *The House Select Committee to Study Government Operations with Respect to Intelligence Activities* and *The Commission on CIA Activities within the United States* (led by the White House) (Johnson 2008: 38 f.). Although an in-depth analysis of all three reports would be of high interest, there is no such academic analysis available. Furthermore, the research literature most commonly refers only to the Church Committee, although all three panels are said to have "produced impressively detailed and thoughtful reports" (Johnson 2008: 39). It would be interesting to explore and compare the different focuses and priorities of the reports (also in terms of word-

period (16 months), it is the best known of all three committees (Johnson 2008: 39). Nevertheless, all committees disclosed several wrongdoings of the CIA, the FBI and the NSA.

With regard to the CIA, the committees exposed that the agency had opened 215,000 pieces of mail of Americans and photographed more than 2.7 million envelopes to get names and addresses. Through this procedure, the CIA generated a database named CHAOS (which was also the operation's name) with 1.5 million names, all alleged subversives (Johnson 2008: 39; Theoharis 2011: 144).

In addition, the NSA-operation SHAMROCK was divulged, which monitored every telegraph message that was sent overseas or received from overseas. Originally created to monitor telegrams sent to the Soviet Union and to examine cables sent by foreign embassies, the NSA began to intercept all telegraph messages that were sent abroad, as mentioned before. NSA officials admitted in hearings to the Church Committee, that just in the last three years 150,000 telegrams had been reviewed monthly. Closely linked to SHAMROCK was the operation MINARET, which was focused on wiretapping within the USA. The communications of more than 1,000 US citizens and 2,400 foreign citizens had been intercepted (Johnson 2008: 39; Schwarz 2008: 25 f.; Theoharis 2008: 144).

Concerning the FBI, the committees disclosed COINTELPRO.[43] Many organizations had been wiretapped, infiltrated or influenced simply because of their political attitudes (particularly civil rights and anti-Vietnam War attitudes). COINTELPRO was founded in 1956 to combat Communists. But the scope expanded over time and included also members of other political groups. Although groups on the extreme right, e.g., the Ku Klux Klan, were also monitored, the program concentrated mainly on leftish groups (especially on the movement headed by Martin Luther King, Jr.). From 1960 to 1974, the FBI held

ing). Unfortunately, it is above the scope of this book to provide such an examination.

43 Also military intelligence services were engaged in COINTELPRO activities. The Church Committee disclosed that military intelligence units collected data about groups involved in subversive activities. The army should have deployed more than 1,500 agents as plainclothes agents to watch demonstrators. All information was shared with FBI officials – which was also against the law (Dycus 2008: 165).

files on one million Americans and investigated against 500,000 subversives (Greenberg 2010: 69; Johnson 2008: 39 f.). Senator Frank Church concluded that fault is to be found "in the long line of Attorneys General, Presidents, and Congresses who have given power and responsibility to the FBI [and other intelligence agencies], but have failed to give it adequate guidance, direction and control" (cited in Greenberg 2010: 95). All in all, three intelligence activities caused alarm: the physical collection of data and the following dissemination of these data as well as the purposeful targeting of individuals without a court warrant (Mills 2015: 202).

Government officials as well as Congress had the capability to detect intelligence activities before. At least with regard to the FBI, House and Senate were informed annually about their activities or had at the very least the opportunity to question the FBI director about measures taken by the FBI. For example, the building of political dossiers was a long known FBI practice. Hoover told Congress in 1960 the Bureau would hold more than five million files. Even so, Congress did not act, among other things, because their members feared the power of FBI director Hoover, who could undermine them with red-bait critic (Greenberg 2010: 95 f.). As Nicholas Katzenbach, a former Attorney General under Kennedy, put it:

> Anyone contemplating an investigation of Mr. Hoover's Bureau would have had to face the strong likelihood that Mr. Hoover would have vigorously resisted. [...] At worst, he would have denounced the investigation as undermining law and order and inspired by Communist ideology. No one risked that confrontation during his lifetime. (Cited in Greenberg 2010: 96)

This shows how strong this counter norm of security was. Even privacy advocates in Congress did not see a discursive opportunity to challenge the security norm. But this changed with the committees on intelligence practices. The reports of the three committees gave rise to broad changes in US intelligence policy. In 1976, Attorney General Edward Levi issued the so-called *Levi guidelines*. From then on, the FBI was prohibited to investigate so-called subversives and was limited to investigate individuals or groups that planned to break the law or could be considered as terrorists. Hence, the political beliefs of targets should not justify an investigation – with only one exception: if the target plans to overthrow the government (Elliff 1984). As a result, FBI investigations dropped from more than 21,000 investigations in 1973 to approximately 4,800 investigations in 1976. Also Congress reached a consensus that legislative steps had to be taken to prevent future abuses of intelligence resources – a sea change. "Most members of the [Church] Committee felt that when the United States ignored its bedrock democratic principles, it risked losing [...] its identity" (Johnson 2008: 42).

Hence, the *Foreign Intelligence Surveillance Act* (FISA) of 1978[44] came into force. With it, primarily domestic eavesdropping activities would be prevented as well as claims by the President for absolute authority to conduct wiretaps in the name of national security. For this, FISA requires a probable cause to make wiretapping legal. Thus, FISA distinguishes *foreign* and *domestic* electronic surveillance (Bedan 2007: 429). Whereas foreign surveillance was not restricted, domestic surveillance was only allowed in cases where it is closely linked to foreign surveillance. So, "the target of surveillance need not be tied to a specific criminal offense. Instead, to satisfy probable cause, the government must show some linkage to a 'foreign power'" (Harper 2014: 1130). It requires an approval in advance by a specially established court (the *Foreign Intelligence Surveillance Court* (FISC)) that has to judge if the target is an agent of a foreign power, a foreign power or an entity that is controlled by a foreign government. This court approval is needed in cases where the surveillance target is a US person who is located in the USA. Thereby, intelligence agencies have to justify the surveillance of individuals and *why* this person is a threat to national security. With the adoption of FISA, Congress superseded the previous major legislative framework governing wiretapping issues, the 1934 Communications Act[45] (Atkinson 2015: 9; Hart 2008: 16; Theoharis 2011: 146). President Carter noted: "It [this bill] will assure FBI field

44 Johnson (2008: 45) provides a good overview of all accountability legislations concerning intelligence agencies in the USA from 1947 until 2006.

45 According to some legal scholars, this loose internationality requirement causes expansive interpretations of this law by state officials. "This setting offers an ideal environment for the government to push statutory and constitutional boundaries. Indeed, recent revelations from Edward Snowden offer confirmation [...]" (Harper 2014: 1124).

agents and others involved in intelligence collection that their acts are authorized by statue and, if a US person's communications are concerned, by a court order. And it will protect the privacy of the American people" (cited in Foerstel 2008: 29).

The spiral model can explain this development very well. The disclosures caused an advocacy process that pushed Congress to create in committees in order to examine the occurrences. At the end of this process Congress established rules that prohibited mass surveillance (and only allowed targeted personal surveillance) and that protected the privacy of the citizens.[46] Although some scholars hold in the light of the history of increasing surveillance of ordinary peoples lifes that "the Church Committee appears to have been a historical accident" (Ashby 2008: 57), this is not true according to the spiral model. It is rather a logical consequence.

4.3. From Reagan to 9/11

The results of the Church Committee and the Levi guidelines, which took effect in 1976, led to a sea change in intelligence surveillance policy. This caused a massive decline in surveillance activities of the FBI, resulting in the cessation of warrantless wiretaps[47]. But this curbing did not last long.

In 1980, Ronald Reagan won the presidential election with a promise to alter Carter's restrained FBI policies and to strengthen the fight against international Communism. Two legal documents cement-

46 Whereas some scholars (Aiken 2008: 50 f.) hold that such a big discussion about the dos and don'ts of intelligence agencies never happened before and are – hence – a good result of democratic power, others (Atkinson 2015) hold that regulations aiming to limit the government's responses to collected information are much more effective than limiting the collection of information generally.

47 Although the wiretapping activities decreased enormously, they never stopped completely. The FBI continued to monitor, e.g., the Black Panther Party and the American Indian Movement. Nevertheless, considering the big picture, the results of the public upheavals in the 1970 s can be seen as successful (Greenberg 2010: 117ff.).

ed this change: Executive Order 12333, issued in 1981, and the *Smith guidelines* administered by Attorney General William French Smith in 1983. The Executive Order allowed the CIA and the Defense Department to conduct spying on American soil in coordination with the FBI. Furthermore, the FBI was allowed to investigate more widely by claiming the target had foreign ties. In addition to that, the term *terrorist* was broadened and also included non-violent activities. However, the Executive Order restricted for the first time foreign surveillance, which had to be "consistent with the Constitution and applicable law and respectful of the principles upon which the United States was founded" (cited in Bedan 2007: 430). This applied to investigations conducted abroad aiming to investigate the behavior of US citizens. Furthermore, the least intrusive investigation technique should be applied (Bedan 2007: 430 f.). On top of that, the Smith guidelines had a stake in this shift towards a national security approach. "Whereas the FBI could start an investigation under the Levi Guidelines only when 'specific and articulable facts' suggested a threat, the Smith Guidelines authorized inquiries 'when the facts or circumstances reasonably indicate' activities involving force or violence" (Greenberg 2010: 122). Smith also stated that the task of the FBI was to anticipate and prevent crime instead of elucidating crime – a first notion of the prevention approach (Theoharis 2011: 148). As a consequence, the FBI started to again investigate a huge number of individuals, claiming that they supported violence and terrorism. The lists of FBI surveillance covered the usual suspects: civil rights groups, anti-nuclear and peace movements, environmental activists as well as lesbian and gay rights groups, black elected officials and Arab Americans. Again, the USA fell from rule-consistent behavior to the state of prescriptive status.

> The Levi Guidelines marked the transition in FBI practice from subversive to terrorist investigations. This reform ended open-ended probes to focus narrowly on groups who were thought to be committing crimes, especially political violence. [...] In a major change, Reagan ushered in a new era of surveillance by broadly linking domestic dissent to terrorism, falsely associating violence with peaceful [...] protest. [...] While all presidents struggle to balance the relationship between national security and constitutional rights, Reagan heavily tipped the scales away from protections for freedom of political expression. (Greenberg 2010: 115ff.)

In the following, the US indeed faced increasing terror attacks on their citizens. In October 1983, almost 300 US Marines were killed by a suicide bomber in their barracks in Beirut – one of the first religious suicide bombings against Americans. Further attacks on US embassies as well as US journalists and academics followed. The administration decided to go on the offensive, causing a new increase of the security norm (Harris 2010: 3, 31).

US intelligence agencies were concerned about the Beirut barrack bombing. Several warnings had been collected by US intelligence agencies but this information did not find its way to the US soldiers on the ground. The agents noticed for the first time, that their information should be shared to gain better results and that they must prevent such attacks. They decided to go this new preventive way secretly, without approval by the Congress, only with presidential directives and executive orders (Harris 2010: 24ff.). This indicates that the actors were aware that the norm of privacy was existent and that for them it seemed to be difficult to push for new laws in Congress.

The Fall of the Berlin Wall ended the Cold War. The communist superpower, the Soviet Union, symbolizing the main threat to the USA, eroded in the aftermath. In Washington, politicians in Congress discussed the so-called *peace dividend*, as it was debated in many Western countries. That meant a shortage of defense and military budget. Although the military spending of the USA decreased in the 1990 s, this did not happen to the intelligence section. One example is the FBI: President Clinton had to explain one of the biggest expansions of the FBI in history. From 1990 to 1999, the FBI budget increased from $1.7 billion to $3.1 billion, with the highest increase in the final three years. In 1997, the FBI employed more than 11,000 agents – the biggest number in history. This increase was justified by the creation of a new enemy: the terrorists (Greenberg 2010: 151ff.).

In 1998, President Clinton appealed to the UN General Assembly to enforce the efforts to combat terrorism:

> Terror has become the world's problem. […] Today, terrorists take advantage of greater openness and the explosion of information and weapons technology. The new technologies of terror and their increasing availability, along with the increasing mobility of terrorists, raise chilling prospects

> of vulnerability to chemical, biological and other kinds of attacks, bringing each of us into the category of possible victim. This is a threat to all humankind. (United Nations General Assembly 1998: 10)

Several terror attacks had cemented the replacement of the communist threat by the terrorist threat: the bombings at the World Trade Center (1993) and in Oklahoma City (1995) as well as the Tokyo nerve gas attack (1995) and the bombing of two US embassies in Africa (1998). Through these attacks the security norm proliferated and made US politicians as well as the US public agree to a fighting-against-terrorism approach, including advocating more spying operations on Americans, although the total amount of terrorist attacks in the USA as well as worldwide decreased.[48] But the US as the sole standing superpower feared that they might become more vulnerable to terrorist attacks, because they remained the prime target for terrorists (Greenberg 2010: 151ff.).

One example occurred in the year 1997. At that time, only two terrorist incidences had occurred in the USA – both small letter bombs. Nevertheless, the FBI stated in the annual terrorism report that the USA would face terror threats in the near future (Greenberg 2010: 161). This threat was combined with the apocalyptic fear of the use of weapons of mass destruction by terrorists. In a report of the same year, the Department of Defense explains:

> As the new millennium approaches, the United States faces a heightened prospect that regional aggressors, third-rate armies, terrorist cells, and even religious cults will wield disproportionate power by using – or even threatening to use – nuclear, biological, or chemical weapons against our troops in the field and our people at home. (Cited in Greenberg 2010: 155)

Another development that was considered a threat was the increasing use of personal computers in the 1980 s and the 1990 s as well as their

48 Terrorist incidents in the whole world were fewer in the 1990 s than in the 1980 s. Indeed, it is questionable why terrorist attacks became the main threat of the US in recent history, especially regarding the numbers of US persons who have actually been killed by terror attacks. Statistically, more Americans die of bee stings or allergic reactions to peanuts than of terrorism (Greenberg 2010: 161; Chesterman 2011: 2).

connection through the World Wide Web[49], which had been invented in 1994 (Lyon 2015: 49). To handle all this new technology, the FBI demanded the power to monitor web traffic as well as access to hard drives. By executive fiat Clinton allowed such snooping. In 1998, the FBI launched a new surveillance system called *Carnivore*. With it, the FBI could spy on e-mails. The system was directly implemented in the system of the Internet Service Providers (ISP) and could search e-mails for certain key words. In addition, it was possible for the FBI to demand that all data be registered to an individual from ISPs. Furthermore, the FBI began monitoring Web browsing, relying on *clickstream data*. These data became available to law enforcement and were not restricted by law (Greenberg 2010: 166 f.).

In addition to that, people started to use cell phones. In 1985, about 200,000 Americans used this new way of telecommunication, five years later already four million used it (Harris 2010: 72). The FBI – like other US intelligence agencies – simply feared to lose the possibility of wiretapping, because communication had changed from the analog to the digital way. They pushed Congress for authorization. In 1994, the Communication Assistance for Law Enforcement Act (CALEA) was adopted. It allowed the FBI to dictate to the phone companies how to create their system's technology. FBI officials wanted them to design their systems in a way that would make them accessible for spying activities.[50] But the negotiations between the FBI and the phone companies failed to reach an agreement on what should be collected because of fierce protests of the telecommunication companies. Hence, a Federal Communications Commission was set in place to judge what is appropriate. The commission ruled in the FBI's favor and also allowed the federal agents to monitor cellular phones and track their location (Greenberg 2010: 168; Schaar 2013: 122). The legal argument of the phone companies had been that the FBI's demands were

49 Because of the Internet structure, most of the information travels through US territory. For information about the history of the Internet and its technical structure, I recommend Bunz (2009) and Sprenger (2015).

50 Laws demanding telephone companies to create their networks in a manner that makes surveillance possible also exist in many other countries in the world, e.g., in Argentina, Australia, Austria, Belgium, Brazil, Canada, Estonia, France, Germany, India, Israel, Malaysia, the Netherlands, New Zealand, Russia, South Africa, Sweden and the United Kingdom (Brown 2013: 206ff.).

unreasonable, because they would enhance the FBI to get much more information than with usual wiretaps. Others questioned the demands by the FBI, because in 1994 FBI agents conducted only 1,154 wiretaps nationwide, mostly for drug investigation (Harris 2010: 79).

The FBI was also continued to mention that – facing a high terrorist threat – encryption technologies enabling criminals to block police and intelligence monitoring needed to be prohibited. Some scholars hold that this debate was created by the government merely to gain more surveillance capacities, referring to the very low degree of this problem. In 1999, the FBI was encountered to encryption only 53 times (Greenberg 2010: 168). Nonetheless, President Clinton issued a presidential directive in 1993 under which the NSA developed a so-called Clipper chip that would be installed in every US phone (a kind of back door for law enforcement and national security purposes). The chip should eavesdrop every phone conversation that was done with such phones (Harris 2010: 75). When the Clipper program became public through a New York Times article in April 1995, business representatives strongly opposed the idea. They claimed that this would hinder foreign customers to buy US products and that company secrets could be revealed by government officials. In the end, the program was dropped (Diffie 2007: 7ff.).

But the intelligence agencies did not only fear the new techniques, they also used them. One of the first departments that used computers to search for information and for profile building was the Army Intelligences Information Dominance Center (IDC) in Virginia. Originally, this unit was created to track cyber attackers of military systems. The analysts developed possibilities to track such people in the cyberspace (Harris 2010: 98). "Their analytic methods relied heavily on information technology 'tools,' specially designed computer programs that processed vast amounts of electronic data and revealed connections among people, places, and activities that the human eye and mind often missed" (Harris 2010: 99). But they quickly realized that these technologies could also be used to track ordinary people thanks to personal information that was delivered by phone metadata and by the open source information on the Internet. At the beginning often neglected, the opportunities of this intelligence unit became present to generals, senior government officials and to some members of Congress (Harris 2010: 99 f.).

Very soon analysts recognized that they had hit a legal wall. While analyzing thousands of web pages, analysts unavoidably collected data on US citizens incidentally (Harris 2010: 111). Nevertheless, in December 1999, the Army's Special Operations Command took notice of the IDC. They needed new techniques to track an upcoming terrorist group, named al-Qaeda. One year before al-Qaeda terrorist had launched attacks on US embassies in Kenya and Tanzania. The Special Operations unit was tasked to map out and dismantle this terror organization. They wanted to study this network like a foreign army and for this they needed active intelligence that showed them where to hit. Hence, the IDC was chosen to help with this task (Harris 2010: 116 f.).

The IDC found many footprints of al-Qaeda around the world, in Europe, North Africa, the Middle East and the Far East – even within the USA. Most of the intelligence agencies were not aware of this huge spread, although most of the IDC's information came from open sources. From now on, the IDC should take the lead in mapping al-Qaeda. The operation was named *Able Danger* (Harris 2010: 120ff.).

But IDC practices had also alarmed government lawyers. Already in 1999, the House Intelligence Committee took notice of the IDC and were concerned about what would happen in case of disclosure (Harris 2010: 113). Here we can observe that actors were indeed aware of the privacy advocates and, therefore, of the existing norm of privacy. Although the lawyers had huge concerns about the program, the IDC continued to work, because this was valuable to *Able Danger's* aim to attack al-Qaeda efficiently. But Rear Admiral Michael Lohr, legal counsel to the chairman of the Joint Chiefs of Staff, early in 2000 noticed that the IDC would "pull together into a single database a wealth of privacy protected US citizens information, in a more sweeping and exhaustive manner than was previously contemplated" (cited in Harris 2010: 124). He observed that the Army must think carefully about how to deal with such a capacity and that this decision should involve the senior level of the Defense Department (Harris 2010: 113ff.).

This would happen in February 2000. Tony Gentry, the top lawyer for the Intelligence and Security Command, ordered the chief analyst of IDC to delete all data relating to US citizens during a 90-day period. All information was deleted (Harris 2010: 130 f.).[51]

In this case, one can consider a process that follows the spiral model – pushing the norm-violating actor, IDC, from step four to the rule-consistent behavior of step five. But the advocates are not INGOs or liberal states, but *inside advocacy actors*. A similar program, called *Thin Thread*, was invented by the NSA, but its use was prohibited in 1999 because of privacy concerns (Electronic Frontier Foundation n.d.b).

At the same time, in the late 1990 s, phone companies like AT&T developed so-called *Packet Scopes*. These made it possible to create a mirror image of all contents of fiber optic cables and to measure and analyze the data that passed through the cables. All the data were stored in a data warehouse of AT&T as long as necessary for record keeping. The companies needed this for record keeping, but at the same time they were concerned about the privacy of their customers. Hence, only the headers of the packets, which showed the address information, were intercepted, not the content. The *Packet Scopes* were fully installed by 1997. From 2001 on, these measures were also used by the NSA (Bamford 2009: 180 f.).

51 The growing interest of US intelligence services and the US Army in the rising Internet structure can be observed in several cases. In 1998, the NSA opened a department for cyberattacks, called the Office of Tailored Access Operations (TAO). It aims to get access to foreign networks through viruses or even through physical break-ins (so-called off-net operations). Since the 1970 s the US conduct such operations, but the foundation of the TAO was the first step toward a professionalization of such attacks (Ruhmann 2014: 41).
Thereby, the USA followed a global trend. In the 1990 s, many countries discovered the possibilities of the cyber space for military and intelligence purposes against foreign countries. States around the world started to develop cyber doctrines: North Korea (in 1998), China (in 1999), Japan (in 2005), and the United Kingdom (in 2009) were among the first. Although the USA has been a pioneer in the practice of cyber attacks against opponents, the first comprehensive US cyber strategy was published in 2011 (Winterfeld & Andress 2013: 31ff.). Nevertheless, the USA has the dubious honor to be the first country that officially announced the first cyber war in history. In March 2016, US minister of defense, Ash Carter, published the first declaration of cyber war. Addressee was the Islamic State. This procedure was seen as the approach to establish the first rules for cyber wars through customary law for want of an international agreement (Kurz 2016).

Besides that, claims for more possibilities of surveillance were raised in the policy arena, because, according to the FBI, many terrorist groups had adopted a leaderless, fragmented structure. To prepare for this, the FBI changed its internal structure to enhance its predictive capabilities (Greenberg 2010: 160). Clinton justified this structural change in March 1999 in a public speech addressing the terrorist threat at that time:

> The only cause for alarm would be to sit by and do nothing to prepare for a problem we know we could be presented with. Nothing would make me happier than to have people look back 20 years from now and say, 'President Clinton overreacted to that, he was overly cautious.' The only way they will say this is if we are overly cautious, if we're prepared, if we can keep bad things from happening. (Cited in Greenberg 2010: 162)

In his words, we can see a new security norm rising: prevention. Although the *de facto* terrorist threat was declining, Clinton justified the government's measures as necessary in order to be prepared for threats that could eventually happen in the future. This pre-emptive approach was the one taken by many Western countries after the 9/11 terror attacks. Nevertheless, during the year 2000 most of the US policymakers viewed the government's anti-terrorism efforts as inadequate and as an overreaction (Greenberg 2010: 156 f.).

In the 1980 s and 1990 s, concerns about serious terrorist threats grew enormously. This led to a proliferation of the norm of security and the preventive approach to security. Nonetheless, and although the security norm led to massive spending by intelligence agencies and to new efforts of surveillance by broadening the term terrorist, the norm of privacy was present and was not weakened by legislative acts, with the exemption of CALEA. Even when intelligence agencies tried to use metadata for the first time, they could only do so in accordance with the norm of privacy. An advocacy process was activated in the mid of the 1990 s when the government sought to install a software to decrypt phones. In the end, this was successful. Advocacy processes of governmental authorities could also be observed in the case of the IDC practices, although the spiral model originally does not include them as advocates.

On the eve of the 9/11 attacks, the norm of privacy was even upheld by President George W. Bush, who stated in an interview on October 6, 2000: "I believe privacy is a fundamental right, and that every American should have absolute control over his or her personal information. Now, with the advent of the Internet, personal privacy is increasingly at risk. I am committed to protecting personal privacy for every American [...]" (cited in On the Issue n.d.).

Despite this, intelligence services were concerned about the new technologies. In December 2000, the NSA stated in a report about the challenges of the 21st century that the increasing volumes of routing data made it more difficult to gain intelligence information. To perform their mission efficiently, the NSA would need to "live on the network" (cited in Electronic Frontier Foundation n.d.b). Thus, they already asked telephone companies to install eavesdropping equipment on their facilities in early 2001. However, the telephone companies refused this request (Bamford 2009: 178).

4.4. After 9/11

The terror attacks in New York and Washington on 11 September 2001 paved the way for strengthening surveillance activities conducted by intelligence agencies – especially in the domestic realm (Nyst/Falchetta 2017: 106).

President George W. Bush argued that the fight against Islamic groups was a global war, labeling it as the *war on terror*: "America and our friends and allies join with all those who want peace and security in the world and we stand together to win the war against terrorism" (2001, cited in Foerstel 2008: 25). This differs essentially from the former approaches that saw terrorism as a matter of domestic law enforcement instead of an issue that needs to be combated with military means (Weisselberg 2010: 71). This point of view did not only cause the invasions into Afghanistan and Iraq but also an extension of domestic mass surveillance (Greenberg 2010: 183).[52]

The security norm proliferated enormously. This can be observed while looking at Vice President Dick Cheney's response to 9/11. In a decree to the CIA two month after the attacks, he advocated the security norm by introducing the *one percent doctrine* saying that all low-probability threats should be treated as a certainty (Greenberg 2010: 184). This kind of thinking caused the implementation of new surveillance measures. Even in public the view was expressed by experts that the Church Committee had weakened the intelligence agencies and that this contributed to the terror attacks (Ashby 2008: 57).

President Bush also agreed to the strengthening of intelligence capabilities in order to implement a new approach to security threats: pre-emption. As Bush stated after the 9/11 attacks,

> new threats also require new thinking. […] If we wait for threats to fully materialize, we will have waited too long. […] We must take the battle to the enemy, disrupt his plans, and confront the worst threats before they emerge. […] Our security will require the best intelligence, to reveal threats hidden in caves and growing in laboratories. (The White House 2002)

Even before 9/11 the shift from a post-crime to a pre-crime society is visible. The trend towards a pre-emptive society – "the rational for broad criminal offences and civil orders that aim to control individuals before they are able to wreck harm upon the community" (Lynch et al. 2010: 5) – was becoming apparent before 9/11 as part of the broader trend to minimize future risks. This trend consolidated and expanded in the course of the post-9/11 world (Mills 2015: 203). But for a comprehensive pre-emptive security approach it is necessary to predict the future. Therefore, intelligence became increasingly important. This has entailed the continuing blurring of borders between the functions of

52 Indeed, similar to previous terror attacks, the 9/11 attacks could have been prevented if information obtained by the intelligence sector would have been pieced together in the right way (Harris 2010: 150). Some scholars (e.g., Cole 2003) hold that with the war on terror a new McCarthyism was launched.

police, military, and intelligence agencies and to a larger extend of surveillance authority (McCulloch & Pickering 2010: 13ff.).[53]

On October 26, 2001, Bush signed the *USA Patriot Act*. In his comment at the signing ceremony he balanced security and privacy issues:

> Today, we take an essential step in defeating terrorism, while protecting the constitutional rights of all Americans. With my signature, this law will give intelligence and law enforcement officials important new tools to fight a present danger. [...] Surveillance of communications is another essential tool to pursue and stop terrorists. The existing law was written in the era of rotary telephones. This new law that I sign today will allow surveillance of all communications used by terrorists, including e-mails, the Internet, and cell phones. As of today, we'll be able to better meet the technological challenges posed by this proliferation of communications technology. Investigations are often slowed by limits on the reach of federal search warrants. (The White House 2001, cited in Foerstel 2008: 46 f.).

The Patriot Act was the direct legal response to the terror attacks that had occured more than one month ago. In Section 802, domestic terrorism is now defined as activities involving "acts dangerous to human life that are a violation of the criminal law of the United States or of any State" (United States Government Publishing Office 2001: 376) and that are intended "to intimidate or coerce a civilian population" (United States Government Publishing Office 2001: 376) or "to influence the policy of a government by intimidation or coercion" (United States Government Publishing Office 2001: 376). This very vague definition gives a great deal of leeway for law enforcement and intelligence agencies to conduct domestic surveillance. Originally, this definition included more than 40 federal crimes comprising computer hacking and malicious mischief. But this plan of the Department of Justice was thwarted by the Senate (Foerstel 2008: 69).

53 This development of blurring the distinction between the functions of intelligence, police and military began already in the 1980 s. While the Church Committee reports still drew a clear line between laws governing domestic (and regulated) law enforcement and foreign (unregulated) national security issues, this distinction was weakened by the Reagan administration for the first time in the war on drugs. By enacting the 1989 Defense Authorization Act, the Defense Department was able to apply US command to watch the drug scene (Diffie & Landau 2007: 137 f.).

Furthermore, the Patriot Act expanded the use of so-called *National Security Letters* (NSL).[54] NSLs are used as a subpoena coming from the administration. Any FBI field officer without authorization by a prosecutor or judge can issue them to a third party, such as telephone companies, Internet providers and financial institutions. NSLs are mainly used for gaining access to electronic communications and the person's proceedings in cyberspace. They can "reveal how and where a person earns a living; how he spends his money; how much he gambles, borrows or pawns; who telephones or e-mails him at home or at work" (Foerstel 2008: 76). The Patriot Act broadened the scope of entities and the scope of parties that are subject to NSLs. This included "eliminating the relevance standard and the need to show specific and articulable facts; expanding the scope of investigations beyond foreign counterintelligence to also include international terrorism or espionage" (Greenlee 2008: 189). A NSL, moreover, is automatically a gag order, which means that the receiver of a NSL, who has to hand over information about a target, is not allowed to make this request public (Foerstel 2008: 76ff.). Again, terrorist threats were used to argue in favor of an extension of NSL use, as a statement by Attorney General Ashcroft shows: "For us to begin to limit the ability to use this law enforcement tool I think would expose the American people to jeopardy because we would have less capacity to enforce the law and keep people safe" (cited in Foerstel 2008: 73).

54 Originally, the Right to Financial Privacy Act of 1978 introduced NSLs regarding to the requests of bank records by federal agents. The law was the reaction to a judgment of the Supreme Court in United States vs. Miller. The Supreme Court held in 1976 that there was "no legitimate expectation of privacy concerning transactional information kept in bank records, and therefore, subpoenas issued by government authorities for such information created no intrusion upon customer Fourth Amendments rights" (Greenlee 2008: 186 f.). Therefore, Congress extended the privacy rights to bank records. Nevertheless, the members sought to balance the right to privacy and the need for law enforcement agencies to obtain such information. They allowed, thus, the access to this information due to a NSL stating that the data holder was an agent of a foreign power. Already in this first version, the NSL was combined with a gag order prohibiting the addressee to inform the target of the subpoena. In 1986, the use of NSLs was extended to telephone company subscriber information and toll bill records by adopting the Electronic Communications Privacy Act (Greenlee 2008: 186 f.).

Section 215 of the Patriot Act amended the FISA Act and allows FBI agents to obtain a search warrant from FISA courts for *any tangible thing* without attesting a probable cause of an illegal act. Agents only have to claim that the demanded information *might* be important for investigating international terrorism or intelligence activities. As Senator Feingold held in the debate on the Patriot Act, "under this provision, the Government can [...] collect information on anyone – perhaps someone who has worked with, or lived next door to, [...] or whose phone number was called by the target of an investigation" (2001, cited in Foerstel 2008: 62). Additionally, gag orders can be issued. Furthermore, roving wiretaps were allowed in Section 206, according to a FISA court warrant. This means that law enforcement officials can follow a person or continue to wiretap this target even when the target changes telephones or communication devices (Foerstel 2008: 52).

The Bush administration's plan was to rewrite the body of law regulating government surveillance. Nonetheless, most of the measures introduced by the Patriot Act had been demanded by intelligence and law enforcement agencies for many years and were not directly related to terrorism issues (Foerstel 2008: 30). Objections had no chance to be heard. Both Republicans and Democrats in Congress "knew that any opposition would be seen as weakness by the American electorate" (Foerstel 2008: 30). This shows that advocacy processes can be stifled by the predominant political climate.

This does not mean that there was no opposition to the Patriot Act at all. Indeed, there was a movement of resistance, which was headed by the ACLU. Soon after the attacks, they published the manifesto *In Defense of Freedom at a Time of Crisis,* calling politicians "to ensure that actions by our government uphold the principles of a democratic society, accountable government and international law, and that all decisions are taken in a manner consistent with the Constitution" (American Civil Liberties Union 2001). More than 150 groups supported the manifesto, including AI, Privacy International and EPIC. Nevertheless, the act of advocacy was ignored in the post-9/11 hysteria; the ACLU's press conference, where the manifesto was presented to the public, was sparsely attended (Foerstel 2008: 31). The prevailing sentiment that terrorist attacks could be adverted by enhanced surveillance powers prevented that this act of advocacy was heard.

The spiral model again fails to explain this turn. It provides no opportunity for something to hamper the advocacy process. Of course, it includes the possibility of low social vulnerability that prevents an actor's advancement to the rank of rule-consistent behavior. But, according to the spiral model a weakening of the social vulnerability by the influence of a competing norm is not possible when a state has already reached the rule-consistent behavior status. But this is what was happening here: The occurrence of a terror attack on US soil weakened the social vulnerability of the USA to the efforts of the transnational advocacy network because the security norm trumped privacy concerns (at least temporarily).

As a matter of course, intelligence and law enforcement agencies immediately started to use their new powers. One of the profiteers was the FBI, which tripled the amount of investigations within a year and quadrupled the requests to eavesdrop on suspected terrorists. On the same day, President Bush signed the Patriot Act, the FBI's Office of the General Counsel sent a memo to all divisions which was almost enthusiastic about the newly gained possibilities of surveillance. The Patriot Act inhibited counterintelligence investigations on US persons that are *solely* based on activities enjoying protection of the First Amendment of the US Constitution, which was highly appreciated by FBI officials:

> Congress inserted this to indicate that the technique will not be used against US persons who are merely exercising constitutionally protected rights. However, it is highly unlikely, if not entirely impossible, for an investigation to be authorized […] that is 'solely' based on protected activities. In other words, all investigations of U.S. persons will likely involve some allegation or possibility of illegal activity […] which is not protected by the First Amendment. (Cited in Foerstel 2008: 42)

In May 2002, a new guideline by Attorney General Ashcroft allowed FBI agents to investigate in *public spaces*. That meant that FBI agents started to monitor chat rooms, bulletin boards and websites without any indication of criminal wrongdoings by the suspects. So-called *fishing expeditions* are conducted to find radical statements and to open further investigations in the case that such statements are found. This extension of surveillance practices was justified with the necessity to prevent another 9/11, although information leading to the 9/11 terror attacks was found in advance but was not analyzed in the right way (Greenberg 2010: 189). Ashcroft claimed that FBI agents had to become better "in detecting terrorist activities to the full extent permitted by the law with an eye toward early intervention and prosecution of acts of terrorism before they occur [to put] prevention above all else" (cited in Theoharis 2011: 149). The new guidelines prompted critical comments in the media, but the majority of the public and Congress accepted this new approach (Theoharis 2011: 149; Greenberg 2010: 190) – the main difference to the 1970 s. This consensus strengthened the security norm.

In 2006, it became public that the FBI used cell phones as tracking devises and eavesdropping tools. Even in 2004, it became public that intelligence agencies were able to activate the microphone of a phone, irrespective if it is on or off. It was expected that this new technique called *roving bug* would be mainly used to spy on UN and foreign government officials (Wheeler 2004). Nevertheless, in 2003 the FBI also started to use this measure to spy on a New Yorker mafioso. This was revealed in 2006, when a US District Court ruled that this practice was legal under contemporary wiretapping law (McCullagh 2006). No advocacy process was activated.[55]

It is obvious that the advocacy process did not work after 9/11. In a way, members of Congress anticipated that they could not act on behalf of the privacy norm directly after 9/11, because of the weak US social vulnerability of that time, but that this would be possible later on. That is why they equipped the most intrusive sections of the Patriot

55 Five years after 9/11, the FBI acknowledged that it did not identify one single al-Qaeda cell within the USA (Greenberg 2010: 205). In addition, in a 2009 report the FBI stated that only five per cent of the leads were credible enough to start further investigations. Between 2005 and 2006, only 19 of 150 FBI international terrorism referrals were charged by the Justice Department (Theoharis 2011: 153 f.).

Act with a sunset provision. After four years, they would lose legal force. Hence, in 2005 debates started in Congress about the reauthorization of the relevant sections, resulting in the USA Patriot Improvement and Reauthorization Act of 2005, which was signed in March 2006.

During the political discussions of the Reauthorization Act, some politicians articulated concerns about too much surveillance power, but the Congress did not follow their arguments, although the debate was lengthy and contentious this time (Foerstel 2008: 193). Nevertheless, the majority of Congress members was convinced of the terror threat argument. As Senator Bill Frist put it: "The Patriot Act expires [...], but the terrorist threat does not" (2005, cited in Foerstel 2008: 180). And deputy Attorney General James Comey said that "especially with some of these tools, if you sunset them again we will never be able to get people to completely believe that the world has changed" (2005, cited in Foerstel 2008: 196).

In the very end, only minor changes were made. The biggest change was made in regard to NSLs. For the first time provisions were put in place for a judicial overview of NSL requests (Greenlee 2008: 194). Regarding Section 215 and NSLs, Congress obtained the right to demand an annual report containing the total number of applications (Foerstel 2008: 187ff.). [56] But the number of sunsets decreased. From 16 sunset provisions only two remained in place, also because Republicans were following the Bush administration's desire to keep all authorities out of the Patriot Act. One of the contested provisions was the sunset division for Section 215 (Foerstel 2008: 197).[57]

56 President Bush did not accept these requirements and rejected them in a signing statement. He reasoned that he could withhold this information as the leader of the executive branch. Nonetheless, there has been a Justice Department Inspector General report in 2007, recording massive abuses of NSLs by the FBI (Conyers 2009: 167).

57 This normalization of extraordinary measures is a trend that can be observed in many countries in the 21st century (McGarrity & Williams 2010: 131ff.). Derogations from certain human rights are allowed according to the ICCPR in cases of public emergency. Only the right to life and the right not be subjected to torture are indispensable (Chesterman 2011: 44 f.).

Besides the legal response to 9/11, illegal responses occurred as well. Originally, to obtain a FISC search warrant, surveillance had to be targeted. But the government, as well as intelligence agencies, wanted to engage in newer approaches of data mining – the opposite of a targeted effort (Mills 2015: 203). In January 2002, the Defense Department's Defense Advanced Research Project Agency (DARPA) was founded in a new department called the Information Awareness Office (IAO). The main target was to develop new tools for anticipating terror attacks and to provide warnings. One of the tools the IAO developed to reach this goal was the Total Information Awareness (TIA) program. TIA aimed to combine *all* the amount of personal information (of US persons and foreigners) that is accessible to all US intelligence services to identify certain structures of behavior and conduct.[58] To put it simply, it was a tool for analyzing big data with regard to certain behavior patterns. As Tony Tether, head of DARPA, opined before a House Committee, "[...] the TIA program is designed as an experimental, multiagency prototype network that participating agencies can use to better share, analyze, understand and make decisions based on whatever data to which they currently have legal access" (2003, cited in Lee 2015: 142). This would help to predict terror attacks, as an official IAO document states (Lee 2015: 143). Albeit private companies had developed such a program before 9/11, it was the first time that the US government was willing to employ such programs to analyze personal information regarding security issues (Lee 2015: 136ff.). In the 1990 s, an approach to create a similar database, called Thin Thread, failed because of privacy concerns. But the *inside advocacy process* did not work completely. Rather one tried to combine both norms.

The notion that the TIA program heavily affected the privacy rights of US citizens and foreigners was clear for the idea generators. That is why the development of privacy protection technologies was one of the top priorities of the TIA. The Genesis Privacy Protection

58 Harris (2010: 151 f.) shows that the war against terror was not the only purpose of this program. Already in its infancy, senior officials were aware of the potential of such a program to ease the decision-making in other fields, especially in the field of foreign policy. Furthermore, people thought about the inclusion of biometric data, such as fingerprints and image scans to TIA, which are not fitting in with the definition of surveillance in this paper.

Program was developed to match this goal. While TIA and intelligence analysts should have free access to the metadata of phone calls or financial transactions, Genesis would deny access to the real name of a target without a court approval. Any access to identifying information would be denied in the first step by Genesis (Harris 2010: 153; Lee 2015: 136ff). General John Poindexter, chief of the IAO and main idea generator of the TIA program, highlighted the privacy issue in his resignation letter in August 2003: "We did not want to make a tradeoff between security and privacy. It would be no good to solve the security problem and give up the privacy and civil liberties that make our country great" (cited in Lee 2015: 147).

The resignation of Poindexter was necessary, because the plans for TIA became public in November 2002 through a *New York Times* article and faced enormous resistance in the aftermath (Lee 2015: 138 f.). The public pressure was so big that Congress stopped TIA in September 2003 by cutting off funding (Lee 2015: 138ff.). But in 2008 the *Wall Street Journal* unveiled that the TIA program was incorporated in a secret NSA program conducting surveillance on the international communication of Americans, the *Terrorist Surveillance Program* (TSP) (Lee 2015: 152).

On October 4, 2001, the Bush administration secretly started a program of warrantless wiretapping for foreign intelligence purposes. The TSP intercepted the communications of US citizens when one party of a conversation was outside the US without a FISA court obligation. The NSA conducted this eavesdropping under the codename STELLARWIND.[59] The President as well as the Attorney General himself reauthorized the program every 45 days. The administration's lawyers justified this program with unchecked legal authority of the President in times of war. According to them, "the President [...] may initiate preventive war without authorization from Congress" (Adler 2008: 99). The deputy Attorney General John Yoo and the legal counsel of Vice President Cheney David Addington were the generators of this justification (Conyers 2009: 146 f.). This is again a main difference to

59 This was the first time since the 1970 s that the NSA conducted domestic surveillance in a broader sense. Before, on US soil they concentrated largely on the surveillance of foreign embassies and missions as well as other missions with a FISC order (Montgomery 2008: 133 f.).

the 1930 s to 1970 s period, when the surveillance activities were clearly illegal. At least this is argued by the President. While presidents and Attorney Generals sometimes enhanced or even ordered these illegal activities, they generally accepted these norms, because they did not try to make new legal approaches to surveillance issues. This changed with the new approach.

A vital change in the behavior and attitude of NSA officials became noticeable immediately after 9/11. As a former NSA-employee put it: "The prior approach focused on complying with the Foreign Intelligence Surveillance Act. The post-September 11 approach was that NSA could circumvent federal statutes and the Constitution as long as there was some visceral connection to looking for terrorists" (cited in Electronic Frontier Foundation n.d.b). Only a few days after the attacks, the NSA drew on the Thin Thread plans to perform contact chaining on metadata.[60] When President Bush signed his order, NSA officials strongly misunderstood it. Indeed, they believed that this order also gave authorization to collect Internet and telephone content and metadata solely of domestic US communications.[61] Consequently, they started to do it. From mid-October on, the NSA approached telecommunication and Internet companies to work with the NSA on this secret program. Many companies agreed voluntarily.[62] During the next two years, the NSA started to build *secret rooms* in the facilities of telecommunication companies to get access to all communications passing through the USA. By the end of 2003, agents of the FBI and CIA joined the program to improve the collaboration between the intelligence agencies (Electronic Frontier Foundation n.d.b).

The Attorney General certified the PSP without assessing the legality of the program, although some administration's lawyers objected

60 The Justice Department had prohibited Thin Thread in December 1999, finding that the examination of metadata is considered as *electronic surveillance* under the FISA (EFF n.d.b).

61 It remains unclear since when the President was informed that in fact also metadata of domestic calls and Internet usage had been collected.

62 In June 2003, one approached company requested the legal basis for this program in a letter to the Attorney General. Three months later, the Attorney General responded that the demands of the NSA were lawful (EFF n.d.).

the plan. But this does not mean that Yoo and Addington were not aware of the breaking of a norm. When the NSA's inspector general, who was informed about the program one year after it had been launched, sought access to the memoranda that served as legal foundation of the surveillance program, Addington rebuffed his request. After Yoo had resigned, the concerns about this program increased in the Justice Department as well. When the President was confronted with the imminent resignation of the level of command of the Justice Department and the FBI, he indulged (Conyers 2009: 148 f.; Electronic Frontier Foundation n.d.b):

In March 2004, the concerns of Justice Department officials became obvious. Deputy attorney James Comey was an opponent of the NSAs activities. One day before Attorney General Ashcroft was hospitalized at a time when one of the regular authorizations was becoming due, Comey told him that the PSP might be illegal. One day later, Comey was the acting Attorney General and denied to sign another 45-day extension of the program. Therefore, White House staff members raced to the hospital to pressure Ashcroft to authorize the bill – which he refused to do. Thus, the White House decided to extend the program without the approval of the Justice Department. This confrontational course caused enormous headwind: Comey as well as several top Department of Justice officials and FBI officials planned to resign. Hence, Bush rescinded the order, and the NSA stopped the mass surveillance program. In the following, FISC was briefed about the program and, after that, in June 2004, gave the first authorization to collect metadata (Conyers 2009: 150; Electronic Frontier Foundation n.d.b).[63]

63 In May 2006, the FISC broadened the scope of Section 215 of the Patriot Act, claiming that the term *business records* was defined as the entirety of a telephone companys database. With it, the court accepted dragnet surveillance by the NSA. This caused President Bush in February 2007 to no longer sign authorizations for the NSA program because the FISC allowed to continue the program indefinitely (Gellmann 2013; EFF n.d.b).

In December 2005, the *New York Times* disclosed the official part of the program[64] after one year of investigation: "[...] the intelligence agency [NSA] has monitored the international telephone calls and international e-mail messages of hundreds, perhaps thousands, of people inside the United States without warrants" (Risen & Lichtblau 2005). President Bush confirmed the existence of the program and defended the program, describing it as a "vital tool in our war against terrorists" (cited in Theoharis 2011: 159). Snowden revealed later that the program also included the collection of metadata for about every phone call and Internet activity of Americans. Furthermore, Bush referenced the permission of Congress, authorizing military operations in the war against terror (Theoharis 2011: 159).

In the aftermath, an advocacy process was activated. The procedures as well as their legal justification attracted the attention of the Justice Department's Office of Professional Responsibility (OPR), which launched an investigation into the President's Surveillance Program (PSP) beginning in 2004 to examine if these rulings had violated the ethical and professional standards of legal profession. In 2009, they published the report stating that especially in the case of Yoo's juridical practice misconduct had occurred. They concluded that "situations of great stress, danger, and fear do not relieve departmental attorney of their duty to provide thorough objective, and candid legal advice, even if that advice is not what their client wants to hear" (cited in Theoharis 2011: 152). The OPR report recommended to refer this case to the bar association for disciplinary actions (Theoharis 2011: 152).[65]

In addition, many lawsuits were opened against the Bush administration and the telecommunication companies, like AT&T, which were

64 Only the collection of metadata of Americans′ conversations with foreigners was revealed – hence, the *official* PSP. Nevertheless, the newspaper reported also about rumors that in some cases the NSA would also capture phone calls of purely domestic nature. That the NSA collects all American's phone calls was revealed by the *USA Today* in May 2006 based on insider reports. Nevertheless, this could not be proved right until the Snowden revelations (EFF n.d.b).

65 President Bush heavily opposed the OPR investigation. Among other things, he denied security clearances to the investigating attorneys to hamper the inquest (Montgomery 2008: 143 f.).

said to have assisted the US government.[66] Many lawmakers and civil liberties groups called for immediate action like Congressional inquiries. Legal scholars and former government officials sent a letter to congressional leaders to express their concerns, thereby especially challenging the legal justification of the President (Montgomery 2008: 124ff.).

Despite this, the advocacy process did not succeed. Although the TSP had caused a lot of public criticism, Congress did not follow up on these concerns. Instead, the members of Congress did not cut the NSA budget (like was done with the TIA program) and they confirmed General Hayden to head the NSA in 2006, who in the same year had stated before Congress: "This [the TSP] is not about intercepting communications between people in the United States. This is hot pursuit of communications entering or leaving America […]. This is focused. It's targeted. It's very carefully done. You shouldn't worry" (2006, cited in Lee 2015: 152).

Besides, Congress enacted the Protect America Act (PAA) and the FISA Amendments Act (FAA) in 2007 and 2008, respectively. The PAA for the first time allowed the surveillance of foreign-to-foreign communication on American soil if there were reasons to believe that the target was outside the USA. Because more than 80 percent of the world's communication is processed through technical infrastructure on US soil, a FISC approval was required for every foreign target. Although the NSA had not followed this rule since the early 2000 s, this rule was officially adopted through the PAA. Furthermore, conversations of US persons with people overseas were exempt from FISC approvals. Hence, the Attorney General and the director of intelligence had to approve the international surveillance operations without attesting that a person was an agent of a foreign power; the FISC only reviewed their decisions. Because the PAA's duration was limited to six months, the FAA was adopted confirming these new measures. Additionally, the FAA excluded all cooperating telecommunication companies from criminal prosecution (Blum 2009: 295ff.; Theoharis 2011: 160 f.).

66 One of these lawsuits was Amnesty International vs. Clapper, filed in 2008. In February 2013, the Supreme Court ruled that the plaintiffs could not prove that they had been monitored by the NSA (EFF n.d.).

Although the Democrats held the majority in both houses in Congress – they are the party that made a major contribution to the accomplishment of the enactment of FISA in the late 1970 s – many of them voted in favor of the proposed bills coming from the White House. They rationalized this decision in public by saying they acted in the name of national security (Montgomery 2008: 152). This led to the FAA, FBI and NSA getting for the first time in history the legal authority to monitor the communications of Americans with persons outside the US (Montgomery 2008: 151).

This reluctance of Congress to oppose the TSP is a subsequent acknowledgement of the Bush administration's procedure. Blum (2009) holds that

> although one can criticize the Bush administration for acting unilaterally and bypassing Congress and FISA, the underlying reasons for the TSP appear genuine and sound. If not, Congress could have taken more aggressive steps to reign in the program once it was revealed instead of passing legislation that retroactively condoned the warrantless surveillance. (296)

Indeed, the loose reaction of Congress this time is the main difference from the situation in the 1970 s, and it highlights "how an obsession over security led it to cede wide latitude to the White House and the intelligence agencies, purportedly to safeguard the nation from potential threats" (Theoharis 2011: 163).

In January 2009, Barack Obama took office. Three years later, the Obama administration stopped the collection of domestic Internet metadata for operational and resource reasons (Greenwald & Ackermann 2013). A few years later, on June 5, 2013, the *Guardian* disclosed that an April 2013 FISC order forced the American telecommunication company *Verizon* to hand over to the NSA on a daily basis all metadata regarding international and purely domestic phone calls for the duration of three months (Greenwald 2013 a).[67] Just a few days later, the *Wall Street Journal* unveiled that such enactments were also given to

67 One may ask if the monitoring of phone call's metadata can be considered as a questionable form of surveillance, because this kind of surveillance does not touch the full content of a phone call (it is not monitored what is said). But this point of view would neglect the huge possibilities of metadata for surveillance. The main

metadata of other American phone companies and Internet providers (Gorman et al. 2013). Further information showed that such enactments were given on a regular basis for years and were reauthorized by the FISC shortly before they expired (Lee 2015: 162; Schaar 2013: 123). Although rumors about such activities of the NSA already existed, government officials denied their truthfulness before the Snowden revelations. In a March 2013 Senate hearing, the Director of National Intelligence, James Clapper, responded when asked whether the question the NSA collected data on millions of Americans: "Not wittingly. There are cases where they could inadvertently, perhaps, collect, but not wittingly" (cited in Greenberg 2013). NSA director Keith Alexander also testified before Congress in March 2012 that an article claiming that the NSA was conducting mass surveillance on Americans was not true. He denied these practices on several other occasions (Cate 2015: 30). This shows that the NSA never intended for this program to become public and that they were aware of the norm of privacy.

The Snowden revelations showed this collection was done under the code name STELLARWIND. Unlike its predecessor Thin Thread, it does not include any privacy protection algorithms (Mills 2015: 204). Later it was disclosed that the metadata of American e-mails were also stored until 2011. Both the bulk phone and the email metadata collection began in late 2001. In 2011, the collection of e-mail metadata was discontinued due to resource reasons, but the bulk phone data collection went on. In cases where the phone metadata of a target should be considered, this is done in two degrees of separation (two hops) (Greenwald 2013 b). Hence, the PSP never really ceased to exist.

It has become clear, from the first warrantless surveillance approach by Roosevelt to the surveillance program authorized by George W. Bush, that national security issues have been the major justification of warrantless eavesdropping.

---

advantage is that metadata are much easier to analyze, process and link than the content of conversations. Furthermore, while content can be encrypted, this is almost impossible with metadata. When metadata are collected over a longer period, they can tell a lot about social relationships, preferences and actual living conditions of an individual (Meister 2013: 229ff.). Some experts (Moechel 2013: 242) hold that with the metadata of a mobile phone much more things can be learned about an individual than with old-school eavesdropping measures.

> Since 9/11, our concept of national security includes protecting domestic locations within the United States. The motivation of national security and the availability of new technology have enabled the surveillance environment in which we find ourselves today, but there has always been a motivation for national security and a thirst to use the new technology of the time. (Mills 2015: 219 f.)

Furthermore, the Snowden revelations also revealed a global mass surveillance approach, which is going to be elucidated in the following. It shows the blurring of the domestic and international spheres with regard to surveillance activities.

4.5. Foreign Surveillance

At the beginning of June 2013, the surveillance program PRISM was revealed. PRISM allows the NSA and FBI to collect personal data from American Internet companies – not only metadata but also content. This data includes "emails, chats, videos, photos, stored data, voice-over-IP, file transfer, video conferencing, logins, and online social networking details" (Lee 2015: 162). PRISM was raised "from the ashes of President George W. Bush's secret program of warrantless domestic surveillance in 2007, after news media disclosures, lawsuits and the Foreign Intelligence Surveillance Court forced the president to look for new authority" (Gellman & Poitras 2013). Congress gave this new authority by adopting the PAA and FAA. Companies voluntarily collaborating with the NSA were free from prosecution. Furthermore, PRISM was justified with the new FISA section 702 allowing electronic surveillance in the USA, as long as no US citizens are intentionally monitored. NSLs were used to obtain the information from companies (Mill 2015: 209ff.). Nevertheless, the privacy protection technology provided by TIA was not included in the TSP by the NSA. The data have been gained indirectly from company servers (Kietz & Thimm 2013: 1 f.; Lee 2015: 162).[68] The distinction between domestic and for-

68 PRISM started in 2007 with collecting data from Microsoft, followed by Yahoo! (2008), Google and Facebook (both 2009), YouTube (2010), Skype and AOL (2011) and Apple (2012) (Lee 2015: 162). The access is an indirect one because the NSA has no direct access to the company servers. Instead, the data are copied to NSA servers where they are analyzed (Moechel 2013: 241).

eign is not existent in the PRISM approach; additionally, data from American citizens (domestic communications) are collected. Although the program officially has to comply with Executive Order 12333, in practice this is not the case (Wright & Kreissl 2015: 14).

Further surveillance programs were disclosed: MUSCULAR has extracted data in bulk from Google and Yahoo! servers overseas without the agreement of the companies. Copying and analyzing the data of the servers have been done without the knowledge of the companies. In addition to that, in joint programs the NSA and the British GCHQ worked together to get access to undersea fiber optic cables around the world. By using intercept probes and physical taps, the intelligence services collect everything that is sent through the fiber optic cables, including phone calls, e-mail messages, Internet history and social network contents. Metadata of this personal data collection are stored for up to one month, the content for three days. With so-called selectors, the intelligence agencies are capable of searching through this data pool and store information on targets (Mills 2015: 210ff.).[69]

The reason why this information is not stored for a longer period is due to the very large storage locations that would be needed for this purpose. As a result, the NSA built a new data center that went online in 2013 and was fully operational in May 2014. It is capable of storing all intercepted data.

Furthermore, the Snowden documents revealed that the NSA used covert implants to get access to computers, smartphones, network servers, firewalls and routers. The malware is able to take over a computers microphone and camera in order to take pictures and record conversations and to collect login details and passwords. While the NSA usually accesses the target machines through the Internet the agency is also able to collect data from machines never connected to the Internet by installing taps (Cate 2015: 32 f.).

All in all, the NSA scandal unveiled three dimensions of surveillance: First, the interception of data in transit that is processed by so-called upstream programs. Second, the access to stored data, as it is done with the PRISM program. This is done in one of three ways: a NSL/FISA warrant, a private agreement between the government and

69 Mills (2015: 210ff.) provides a list of all revealed surveillance programs in 2013.

the company; or by hacking into the systems (Mills 2015: 218). A third layer is the installation of spyware on personal devices like computers or smartphones (Lyon 2015: 18ff.). As a result, the distinction between mass and targeted surveillance has blurred. "If data are sought on a mass basis […] with a view to identifying who might be a 'person of interest,' the point at which 'mass' becomes 'targeted' surveillance is fuzzy at best" (Lyon 2015: 22). This goes so far that intelligence agencies insisted after the Snowden disclosures that the mere mass capture of data without later intervention could not be defined as surveillance (Lyon 2015: 41 f.). Another two spheres that are blurred are the distinction between state surveillance and surveillance conducted by companies, since the US intelligence agencies have direct access to the data collected by US companies (Lyon 2015: 29).

This infrastructure comes very close to a global mass surveillance of as many individuals as possible. Today, the NSA intercepts two million types of communication per hour (Lee 2015: 159). This is not the first time that such an approach of global mass surveillance is conducted. There is one predecessor: a program called ECHELON.

ECHELON was also capable of performing a total surveillance approach of virtually all kinds of technical communication. The program, set up in 1971 and operationalized by the NSA under permission of the intelligence alliance *Five Eyes*[70], was "worlds away from the popular conception of the old wiretap" (Goos et al. 2015: 57) by intercepting all communications that were processed over satellite and captured all messages that were relevant for national security. First rumors about this program already existed in the late 1980s when whistleblowers and journalists reported about it. This made the EP's Science and Technology Options Assessment committee scrutinize and report about ECHELON in 1999, leading to an EP report in July 2001 that officially revealed the program. The report was concerned about the ECHELON

70 The partnership in SIGINT between the USA, the UK, Australia, Canada and New Zealand is known as *Five Eyes* and emerged in 1947. The initiating agreement, named UKUSA Agreement, was actually an agreement between the UK and the US, but as the UK colonies became independent, they joined the coalition (Bedan 2007: 435).

program and stated, "any interception of communications represents serious interference with an individual's exercise of the right to privacy" (EP 2001). Nevertheless, the advocacy network could not push the USA and its Five Eyes allies to respect the privacy norm. The reason for this was a considerable shift in public perception: The 9/11 attacks, committed only two months after the EP's report was published, made the public focus on security instead of privacy issues. Albeit the actual target of ECHELON was the interception of the Soviet Union's communication and their satellite states, the program continued after the end of the Cold War – also to conduct business espionage against the Europeans (Bedan 2007: 435 f.). Documents revealed by Snowden showed that the program is still active today, although most of the world's communication is transferred through fiber optic cables (Rudl 2015).

The NSA development of new approaches of surveillance in the 1990 s was due to the fact that more and more communications were transmitted by fiber optic cables and not via satellite. Fiber optic cables transmit signals much faster than microwaves, which was important in the face of the development of the Internet and rising communications via Voice over Internet Protocol (VoIP). The global network of fiber optic cables had one crucial point: the so-called *switches,* "central nodes and key crossroads where millions of communications come together before being distributed to other parts of the country. [...] Like border crossings, they are the points of entry for all international cable communications" (Bamford 2009: 176 f.). More than half a dozen switches had been installed on both US coasts, processing 80 percent of all international communications (Bamford 2009: 175ff.). This led to the development of the PRISM program.

But is the surveillance of foreigners on foreign soil a breach of the norm of privacy? Indeed, US law does not prohibit foreign surveillance. Until the 1970's, foreign intelligence operations were not regulated. And even after investigations of the Church Committee following the Watergate scandal and the adoption of the FISA Act, no privacy protection mechanisms had been installed for intercepting communication of two foreigners on foreign soil (Johnson 2016: 231ff.). "This decision was not a mistake. Rather it was a deliberate policy choice, and the norm for foreign intelligence programs worldwide" (Johnson 2016: 234).[71] The same is true with view respect to international law. Because of the widespread practice of espionage, "there are no specific international law norms that prohibit or regulate espionage" (Peters 2017: 163).[72]

But do the non-prohibition of espionage in the international realm and the missing domestic rules on foreign intelligence automatically deny the right to privacy of non-citizens on foreign soil? Since the NSA Affair, legal scholars have been debating this question. With regard to the US constitution, some scholars (Miller 2017) conclude that it provides no rules "that can be said to clearly and definitely resolve the question of its application to foreigners or beyond Americas territorial jurisdiction" (92), others (Walen 2017) argue that there is no case law on constitutional rights clearly prohibiting the extension of such rights to nonresident aliens (NRA). "[...] in the in the wake of Boumediene v. Bush, the jurisprudence has moved in favor of extending constitutional protections to NRAs" (Walen 2017: 283).

Whereas the scope of the constitution's application is still a matter of debate, the evidence seems much more clear in view of international law. The ICCPR, which formulates the right to privacy (and especially to informational privacy (Vöeneky 2017: 500)) in Article 17, has extraterritorial validity, because all singers declare to guarantee this right to subjects to its jurisdiction (Vöeneky 2017: 501 f.; Peters 2017: 151ff.). "[...] one has to conclude that a state's jurisdiction is implicated even if a state merely exercises factual power on the territory of a nonstate or third party. Factual power is exercised in the conduct of espionage on the territory of another state" (Vöeneky 2017: 501 f.). Hence, if a state wants to restrict or limit the right to privacy of foreigners on foreign soil, this must be – according to the ICCPR – pro-

71 The question remains, if the concepts of territoriality and nationality are still useful tools to guide intelligence practices in times of Internet traffic traveling the whole globe before reaching its destination (Johnson 2016: 235ff.).

72 Nevertheless, there are other treaties and principles of international law that have been violated by the USA. According to Peters (2017: 164ff.), the USA "breached the law of diplomacy by conducting surveillance activities at and through embassies" (167) and they violated the principle of Westphalian sovereignty.

portionate and in order to reach a legitimate aim (Vöeneky 2017: 502; Peters 2017: 153ff.). In addition to this, "the ICCPR protects persons against discrimination" (Peters 2017: 162), which is why the USA owes every person – US citizen or not – equal protection of the international right to privacy (Peters 2017: 162 f.).

This interpretation of international law is not new. Already in 1988, the UN Human Rights Committee clarified that any kind of electronic surveillance and wiretapping of conversations violates international law (Peters 2017: 148).

The question remains if the US foreign surveillance activities are legitimate and proportionate – and, hence, comply with standards of international law. Especially since 9/11, the USA feel threatened by terrorists. But "a shocking insight is that many of the surveillance methods implicated by the NSA programs [...] are not very effective at exposing the plans of terrorists" (Peters 2017: 162), which results in a "deep and significant intrusion on the right to communications privacy" (Peters 2017: 162), generating little benefit (Peters 2017: 162). Therefore, the foreign surveillance activities of the USA exposed by Edward Snowden can be considered as a norm violating behavior.

As shown up to this point, "security [has become] a key driver of greater surveillance" (Lyon 2015: 31), not only since 9/11. How this relates to the spiral model will be scrutinized in the next section.

4.6. The USA and a Comprehensive Spiral Model

Is the spiral model a useful tool to explain the degradation of a human rights norm? By illuminating the history of mass surveillance, it became clear that the five steps of the spiral model are not sufficient to explain the norm regression in the USA.

The regress of a human rights norm does not happen in the same way it emerges. While the spiral model is capable of covering the secret violation of a norm by government authorities (the step from rule-consistent behavior to the prescriptive status), the five categories of the spiral model do not fit to explain further norm regressions, because the next step (from the prescriptive status to the status of tactical concessions) would include the withdrawal of international treaties and national law that includes the human rights norm. On the contrary, it seems that the withdrawal from law might be a very advanced step of norm regression. The history of the struggle between the norm of privacy and the norm of security in the USA shows that the spiral model is not capable of explaining the developments.

Furthermore, the spiral model is not capable of explaining why the advocacy processes are not successful in every case. This was most obvious after 9/11: International advocacy groups joined domestic NGOs to prevent the renunciation of human rights norms. According to the spiral model, this can only be explained with the lower social vulnerability of the norm violating state. However, the general political climate seems to influence the effectiveness of the advocacy process as well.

Nevertheless, a certain structure can be observed that summarizes the developments in the USA, which can be theorized in a second spiral. To get a comprehensive model of how states are prevailed to comply with a norm and how this development is inverted, such a second spiral seems necessary. By reference to the case study presented in this chapter a *spiral B* can be proposed. The different stages are not selective but fluent, as it is the case with the original spiral model. A certain framework can be deduced from the development of mass surveillance in the USA; it consists of five steps – similar to *spiral A* of the spiral model.

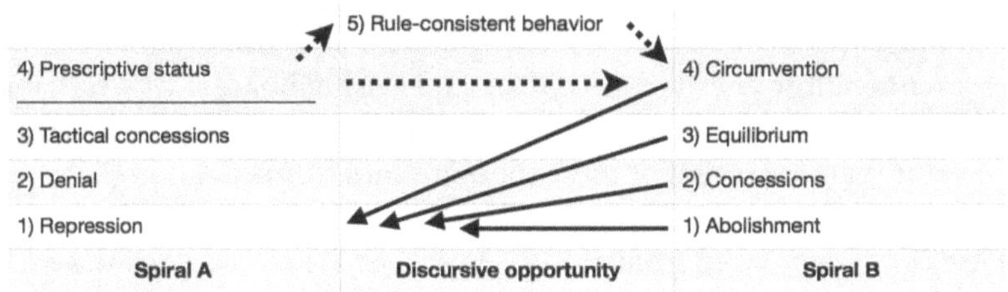

Fig. 1) The Comprehensive Spiral Model

5) *Rule-consistent behavior:* This phase is equivalent to step five of the original spiral model. A state has ratified international treaties, accept-

ing the human rights norm, and acts on behalf of this norm. Furthermore, the state has included this norm in domestic jurisdiction and acts on behalf of this norm without questioning it.

Since the USA began to violate the privacy norm from the moment of its juridical implementation, the country has literally never reached this status. Only for a very short time after the Church Committee hearings this status can be assumed.

4) *Circumvention:* Some state authorities or politicians start to act in a way that contradicts a human rights norm. Their behavior is led by a counter norm that objects the human rights norm. Nevertheless, a majority of the public as well as a majority in the political arena does not support this counter norm. Attempts to implement the counter norm in domestic or international jurisdiction fail. Nevertheless, the actors advocate the counter norm in public and a first diffusion of the counter norm sets in. Because persons and authorities acting on behalf of the counter norm are aware of the prevailing political climate, they try to conceal their acts. By doing this, they show awareness of the prevailing human rights norm: They hide their actions to circumvent the human rights norm, because they fear future prosecution and because they know their actions are not accepted. The more the counter norm spreads, the more actors acting on behalf of this norm feel vindicated and continue their secret acts or extend them. Not until the human rights norm is dead, unrestricted behavior on behalf of the counter norm is possible. Furthermore, the violation of the human rights norm does not necessarily have to become public. *Inside advocacy actors*, i.e., actors inherent to the state level, like supervising boards, civil servants (e.g., lawyers) or individual politicians, can prevail the norm violating procedures and ensure that these measures are stopped.

In reference to the history of mass surveillance in the USA, this phase can be observed from the early years of Roosevelt until the early 1950s and from the Reagan administration until the 1990s. Roosevelt's justification of surveillance for the *defense of the nation* developed in the Truman era into a comprehensive approach to *national security,* but the security norm did not challenge the privacy norm considerably. And although surveillance measures were extended in the Reagan years because of security concerns, the security norm was inasmuch not a considerable part of public discourse, because the privacy norm was not challenged publicly. Both periods show an existence of the counter norm of security and politicians and authorities acting on behalf of this norm. Although terms like *subversive* and *terrorist* were shaped and broadened over time to justify the departure from the human right to privacy in the name of national security, Congress did not pass any laws that reduced the validity of the human right to privacy. The attempts by Roosevelt, Hoover and Celler to push Congress to adopt such laws failed. Instead, they had to hide their actions, which did not comply with the privacy norm. Nevertheless, albeit a counter norm was present the majority of the public and state actors were not convinced to cut privacy rights in favor of gaining security.

3) *Equilibrium:* This phase is characterized by finding a compromise between both the human rights norm and the counter norm. The counter norm continues to spread and resonates significantly. Nevertheless, both norms are now more or less equally acknowledged and represented in public and in the political arena. This can lead to the enactment of laws or treaties that try to combine the requirements of the two norms. Another possibility to reach equilibrium is to suspend the human rights norm temporarily. This shows that the counter norm is only accepted in a specific situation – e.g., in case of an emergency. This does not have to be against international law. In case of the privacy norm, a temporary suspension of this human right is acceptable and legal in special situations.

Generally, the human rights norm is not rejected. In this phase, it is less likely that internal advocacy actors initiate advocacy processes, because actions on behalf of the counter norm are to a certain extent legal, and many more people on the state level are advocating the counter norm, in this case: the norm of security. Hence, it is less likely that inside advocacy actors initiate spiral A. Additionally, the successful initiation of the spiral is not granted, because the social vulnerability of a state often decreases with the adoption of a contradicting norm.

This phase can be observed in the case study from the 1950 s (the adoption of the Omnibus Crime Control and Safe Streets Act) until the early 1970 s, when an advocacy process initiated by the press and NGOs led to a sea change in the intelligence policy of the USA and pushed the state to a rule-consistent behavior, and from the mid 1980 s until 2007.

With the Coplon case, the security norm spread significantly in the apparatus of state. The discussions in Congress in the 1950 s about the legalization of wiretapping are an example of the noticeable resonance of the security norm in the public space. This was followed by the adoption of the Omnibus Crime Control and Safe Streets Act in 1968. In retrospect, the Act was a very naïve try to combine both norms: It was a commitment to the right to privacy and – by allowing wiretapping for reasons of national security – a commitment to the norm of security.

In the 1980 s, the USA again entered the stage of equilibrium. Although the Huston plan was almost a step towards the stage of concession, it was not implemented for fear of an advocacy process. In the Clinton era, the security norm resonated in public in the form of an advocacy process (by the government) in favor of a preventive security state. The adoption of the CALEA is an expression of it. Other initiatives, like the Clapper program, failed. However, the events of 9/11 pushed the security norm enormously. But the Patriot Act was not a general renunciation of the right to privacy. Many senators and representatives were aware that they only wanted to limit the right to privacy and other civil and human rights temporarily to respond to the terrorist threat effectively. That is why many provisions curtailing privacy were equipped with sunset provisions. Furthermore, although the counter norm diffuses at the state officials' level, there still exists a considerable amount of officials upholding the human rights norm. This is symbolized by the dispute between the Bush/Yoo camp and the Comey camp in 2004.

An attempt to combine both norms was not only made by jurisdiction but also by the intelligence agencies. The development of TIA is an example of the development of a surveillance system that complies with the privacy norm. After the stoppage of the IDC through inside advocacy actors, TIA was developed as a system that tries to combine both norms, but it did not survive the activation of the spiral model in the aftermath of the disclosure by a newspaper article.

Even public statements showed the equal awareness of both norms. In the signing ceremony of the Patriot Act, Bush noticed that this act would defend both security and civil liberties of Americans.

2) *Concession:* By entering this phase, advocates of the counter norm have gained mastery. Concessions are made to them by the implementation of the counter norm in legislation at the expanse of the human rights norm. The laws and treaties providing the basis for the human rights norm are restricted – but not completely canceled. For certain situations or individuals the human right is not valid any more. The social vulnerability of a state further decreases. State authorities are increasingly acting on behalf of the counter norm. In public discourse, the counter norm is generally accepted.

The USA reached this phase with the adoption the PAA in 2007 and of the FAA one year later. The revelations from the end of 2005 did not led to rule-consistent behavior. Instead, PAA and FAA restricted the right to privacy as being valid only for the domestic communications of Americans. Intelligence agencies began to work on behalf of these new laws. Furthermore, phone companies could not be sued for any actions violating the privacy norm. The acceptance of secret surveillance activities on Americans by the FISC can also be classified at this stage (although it happened already in 2004), because it shows that arguments in favor of the counter norm (in this case, by the NSA) influences decisions of judges and actions of human rights oversight mechanism (!) enormously (in this case, of the FISC court).

1) *Abolishment:* In this phase the human rights norm is dead. Treaties or laws advocating this norm are abandoned. State officials officially deny the validity of the human rights norm, and state authorities stop acting on behalf of the human rights norm completely. No illegal and secret actions on behalf of the counter norm are necessary anymore, because the human rights norm is overcome.

This phase was developed in theory and without evidence of the case study on the USA. Nevertheless, this would be a logical consequence of this development. At least theoretically, the Snowden revelations could cause the USA to enter this phase – similar to the development in 2007, when revelations did not lead to a behavior that is more rule-consistent. In the public discussion, it is theoretically possible that the privacy norm is further weakened by normative arguments on behalf of the security norm and that the existence of the surveillance programs unveiled by Snowden are accepted in the end. How likely this is going to happen, will be explored in the next chapter.

All in all, this second spiral can explain the development of a state from complying with human rights to differing from this norm. Nevertheless, it is merely a first attempt to theorize this evolution. This second spiral has to be verified by further case studies, as a matter of course. Of peculiar interest would be the question whether this model also applies to *strong norms* like the prohibition of torture.

It is questionable if this model can be used to explain the international condition of a human rights norm. The programs ECHELON and PRISM, conducted by a multilateral intelligence cooperation network led by the USA, can merely be considered as a first attempt to circumvent the norm of privacy (spiral B, step 4, 'circumvention'). The diffusion of the security norm at the international level did (at the time of writing) not influence existing international human right treaties with regard to weakening the norm of privacy. Prima facie, this seems to be in line with the findings of McKeown (2009: 11) whereupon a norm is first encountered in the domestic arena, and afterwards this development reaches the international level. But there are also counterarguments to that: The norm security has widely spread in the last decade at international level, which would actually demand to classify the condition of a norm as weaker than the stage of circumvention. Nevertheless, because the spiral model was developed to explain domestic policy changes, problems to explain the norm regression in the international sphere are not surprising.

Furthermore, the proposed framework fails to explain the interdependencies of state actors and advocacy networks that are fundamental to the original version of the spiral model. It is beyond the scope of this paper to illuminate the advocacy actors in every single phase; instead, the state behavior was central to this case study. This has to be done by further research. Merely one conclusion can be drawn with regard to this: The level of non-compliance influences the mechanisms of social actions, particularly *coercion* and *persuasion*. First, the higher the degree of non-compliance, the harder it is for domestic and international advocacy groups to enforce human right norms legally. Once the domestic law is changed, it is more difficult for advocacy groups to enforce a human right in court. Second, with the increasing acceptance and influence of a counter norm to the policy of a state, it gets harder to convince a state to comply with a human rights norm. Mostly, this goes hand in hand with the diffusion of the counter norm in the public.

The original spiral model has to be expanded by one more facet. As the case study shows, there are some examples where the transnational network is activated but failed to push the state to a rule-consistent behavior. The original spiral model does not provide an explanation for this. As the case study showed, it is very often the political climate that prevents a successful iteration of the spiral. To include this possibility in the spiral model, it is necessary to add one more scope condition: the discursive opportunity. Whether an advocacy process is successful or not, is dependent on the existence of a *window of discursive opportunity*[73]. The original spiral model merely contains the scope condition of

73 The theory of *discursive opportunity* has its roots in the concept of *political opportunity*. This concept wants to highlight that the success of social movements is not only dependent on the actors and actions of social movement groups but also of the political framework and circumstances in which the movement acts. In other words, a political opportunity refers to "aspects of the political system that affect the possibilities that challenging groups have to mobilize effectively" (Giugni 2009: 361). Charles Tilly (1978) made the most important contribution to make this approach circularize in research literature, because he was the first to come forward with a comprehensive approach. Nevertheless, this approach was criticized enormously for its vagueness; it was in danger "of becoming a sponge that soaks up virtually every aspect of the social movement environment" (Gamson & Meyer 1996: 275). In response to this critique, scholars started to further specify the concept. One result was the development of the discursive opportunity approach. It purports that there is "a discursive side relating to the public visibility and resonance as well as the political legitimacy of certain actors, identities, and claims" (Giugni 2009: 364). This is meant when I refer to discursive opportunity here.

social vulnerability. However, it is not only the social vulnerability of the state but also of the society and public that decides about the success of an advocacy process. The question if spiral A can be activated, if the advocators are able to pressure a state to a rule-consistent behavior will be dependent on the prevailing discourse in the public domain. A temporary change in discourse in favor of the human rights norm triggered by revelations or public discussions about new laws (tipping point) is necessary to guarantee the success of spiral A. Thereby, the comprehensive spiral model can explain that norm-violating procedures survive their disclosures in cases where such a discursive opportunity is not existent (a main point of criticism to the spiral model by McKeown (2009: 10)).

At every stage of norm regress, discursive windows of opportunities (like exposures of norm violations) can emerge and be used to activate the spiral A. This is symbolized in the chart by the intact arrows. However, if the advocacy network is not successful in pressuring the violating state to the prescriptive status, the norm regress is not stopped and can continue. This is symbolized by a line between the steps of tactical concession and prescriptive status. If the prescriptive status is reached, two possibilities exist: the further development of rule-consistent behavior as well as the immediate challenge of a norm by counter norm entrepreneurs, which would directly lead to a stage of circumvention. These two possibilities are symbolized by the broken arrows in the chart.

Whereas this chapter has focused on how the development of non-compliance with a human rights norm is possible, the next chapter will explore the actions of the advocacy network after the Snowden revelations and, hence, will focus on the second research question. Following the comprehensive spiral model, the revelations give the opportunity to activate *spiral A*. The next section will show if this happened.

5. Norm Defense: The Advocacy Process after Snowden

This chapter is going to throw light on the advocacy process that followed the Snowden revelations. It will explore what kinds of mechanisms and modes of social action have been used by human rights advocates to pressure the USA to comply with the human right to privacy. The spiral model differentiates four such modes: coercion (use of force or legal enforcement), changing incentives (sanctions and rewards), persuasion (by discourse) and capacity building.

The main contributors to the international human rights regime should be explored: liberal states, IOs, and (I)NGOs. As a matter of course, not all advocates can be scrutinized here; instead, I focus on a few of them. When I look at the liberal states, I will focus on the states that advocated the right to privacy the strongest. Regarding the IOs, the behavior of the three most important actors will be analyzed: First of all, the UN is the organization that has made the biggest contribution to the establishment of human rights in the international system. Hereafter, the EU as well as the CoE will be scrutinized. As mentioned in the third chapter, they have both been relevant actors in the establishment of the right to privacy. Last but not least, NGOs should be highlighted. AI is one of the biggest international human rights organizations and, therefore, a good example to use to explore the advocacy process at the international NGO level. Although the behavior of all actors will be scrutinized separately, their activities are interdependent as a matter of course (Nyst/Falchetta 2017: 109).

5.1. Liberal states

The strongest commitment to privacy has been made by Brazil and Germany (Nyst/Falchetta 2017: 105). Together, both initiated a UN resolution on the right to privacy in the digital age.

Brazil's president Dilma Rousseff canceled a September 2013 visit to the USA and instead delivered a speech at the UN, which was the most direct response of a state leader in public. Rouseff noted:

> The right to safety of citizens of one country can never be guaranteed by violating fundamental human rights of citizens of another country. […] In the absence of the right to privacy, there can be no true freedom of expression and opinion, and therefore no effective democracy. […] We expressed to the Government of the United States our disapproval, and demanded explanations, apologies and guarantees that such procedures will never be repeated. […] Brazil, Mr. President, will redouble its efforts to adopt legislation, technologies and mechanisms to protect us from the illegal interception of communications and data. My Government will do everything within its reach to defend the human rights of all Brazilians and to protect the fruits borne from the ingenuity of our workers and our companies. The problem, however, goes beyond a bilateral relationship. It affects the international community itself and demands a response from it. Information and telecommunication technologies cannot be the new battlefield between States. Time is ripe to create the conditions to prevent cyberspace from being used as a weapon of war […]. For this reason, Brazil will present proposals for the establishment of a civilian multilateral framework for the governance and use of the Internet and to ensure the effective protection of data that travels through the web. […] Harnessing the full potential of the Internet requires, therefore, responsible regulation, which ensures at the same time freedom of expression, security and respect for human rights. (Rouseff 2013: 158 f.)

Rousseff argued on the basis of human rights. Brazil has acted on their notice and adopted new legislation to strengthen privacy protections for their own citizens. In 2014, Rousseff signed a *Civil Rights Framework for the Internet* into law that requires the government to decide if an Internet provider is acting fairly and protecting consumer's privacy. Among other things, Rousseff promoted legislation forcing global Internet providers to store the customer data of the Brazilians inside Brazil. In February 2014, Brazil and the EU decided to build their own undersea cable between Portugal and the Brazilian coast. Additionally, Brazil hosted a global multi-stakeholder meeting, NETmundial, where participants discussed the future of Internet governance (Fidler 2015 a: 157; Wright & Kreissl 2015: 25 f., 29; Sales 2015).

In Germany, concerns about mass surveillance of the communication of Germans were also huge. They caused an increased effort to strengthen the right to privacy at the international level, which found expression in the support of a UN resolution. But also at the bilateral level, Germany delivered consequences. The German government terminated an intelligence treaty with the USA from the Cold War era. Furthermore, Germany tried to negotiate a so-called *no-spy agreement* with the USA and minimized the cooperation of German and US intelligence agencies. The government did not renew the contract with the US telephone company *Verizon* because of security concerns (Fidler 2015 a: 160; Connolly 2015).

Nevertheless, German Chancellor Angela Merkel did not push publicly for stronger protection of privacy rights. She tried to minimize the incident and reminded the Germans of the important role of the USA in post-War German history. After it became public that the NSA had intruded on her own privacy by monitoring her phone, however, she proved to be more concerned in public (Wright & Kreissl 2015: 30).[74] Her strongest public reaction was: "Spying on friends – that does not work" (Roth & Gathmann 2013).

In 2014, the German Parliament, the Bundestag, launched an investigative committee on the NSA affair. The result was a research report published in June 2017, stating that the USA did not conduct mass surveillance, because their activities had not been executed without probable cause (the parliamentary opposition dissented from this assessment) (Deutscher Bundestag 2017: 1214ff.; Biermann 2017 b). The main findings of the investigative committee had been the collaboration of the German intelligence agencies, mainly the *Bundesnachrichtendienst*, with intelligence agencies of the *Five-Eyes* member states (Biermann 2017 a). As some scholars hold (Peters 2017: 168 f.), these surveillance activities of German (and other European) intelligence agencies – as they were brought to light by the committee

74 Besides that, the Bundestag as well as a few other Parliaments in the world (Canada, United Kingdom) launched inquiries. In all countries the committees faced the refusal to cooperate by foreign and domestic officials and, partly, their own governments (Gill 2015: 84; Gebauer et al. 2013).

– probably violated the European Convention on Human Rights by "concluding bilateral agreements with the United States, by tolerating US activities, and by engaging in surveillance programs themselves" (Peters 2017: 169).

Because of the intermingled relationship of the Bundestag and the German government, which is typical of parliamentary democracies, the success of this committee largely depended on the parliamentary opposition (Miller 2017: 72 f.). Nevertheless, it seems that the parliamentary opposition succumbed in the debate about the consequences of the findings of the inquiry: In October 2017 the Bundestag adopted a new intelligence law establishing new oversight mechanisms but also – according to critics – largely legalizing the wrongdoing of the German intelligence agencies (Biermann 2017 c; Heißler 2017).

Besides Germany, other European states were concerned as well. France's Minister of Foreign Affairs, Laurent Fabius, noted that this kind of espionage would be not acceptable. The reaction of the United Kingdom was relatively muted. The Information Commissioner stated that the conduct of the USA might contradict European data protection law (Wright & Kreissl 2015: 9 f.).

There were plenty of other states complaining about the NSA surveillance measures, not only liberal states with rule-consistent behavior. However, this does not automatically result in a commitment to privacy. One example is a statement of the Chinese National Ministry of Defense demanding that the USA to stop surveillance activities.

> For a long time, the relevant agencies of the United States have relied on its advanced technology and infrastructure to carry out large-scale, organized cybertheft, bugging and monitoring against foreign politicians, businesses and individuals. These facts are known to all. The hypocrisy and double standards of the United States regarding Internet security issues have been abundantly obvious from WikiLeaks to the Snowden affair. The Chinese military is a serious victim of this kind of US conduct. [...] China demands that the United States [...] immediately stop such activity. (Chinese National Ministry of Defense 2014: 165)

It is remarkable that the Chinese Ministry of Defense complained about US surveillance practices without even mentioning the word *privacy*. There is talk of *Internet security* instead. This makes sense when it comes to the prioritization: Cybertheft as well as spying on politicians is first mentioned. Only afterward, the mass surveillance on individuals is expressed. Although many states are concerned about the US surveillance practice, one can assume that a big part of international complaints is driven by the strategic interests of those states (against US interests of cyber security matters) instead of a true commitment to the human right to privacy (Fidler 2015 a: 164).

All in all, the reaction of liberal states was considerably weak. This is due to both lacking of political will and missing or inappropriate tools to punish the norm violation by the USA. First of all, two of four modes of social action are not available to liberal states or inappropriate in use. Since the USA is a consolidated democracy and, thus, is not lacking limited statehood, capacity building is not appropriate. Furthermore, it would be questionable what kind of capacities should be enhanced, as the definition of privacy and how to protect this human right are highly controversial even between European states. Coercion is also not a possible tool to use. The use of military force would be inappropriate, because mass surveillance is not a classical military attack. On the other hand, there are no supranational legal institutions (e.g., like the International Criminal Court) available that would be responsible for punishing the violation of the right to privacy within the means of law.

Therefore, the only modes of social action, which are possible, are persuasion and changing the incentives for the violating state. However, no state imposed sanctions against the USA or used other measures to influence the utility calculation of the USA in a positive or negative way. Although many states reacted with domestic consequences (terminating contracts with US companies and intelligence agencies or adopting laws to enhance domestic privacy regulation), these measures did not so much aim for influencing the utility calculations of the USA as at minimizing the US power base regarding the Internet. The planned installation of an undersea fiber optic cable between Portugal and Brazil is a good example of it.[75] This action does not aim to change US behavior but their possibilities of mass surveillance.

To make matters worse, domestic consequences are not necessarily a pure commitment to privacy. For example, albeit the new Internet law in Brazil was adopted with the intention to protect the privacy of Brazilian Internet users, Sales (2015) observes that the Snowden revelations were used by the Brazilian government to increase state control over the Internet. This action does not constitute a confession to privacy as such, because a lot of authoritarian countries, like China or Iran, also have huge control over the Internet (Krieger 2014: 346) and do not use this power to enhance privacy protection. The new German intelligence law is another example. Hence, one has to await further developments and the usage of the new state competences by Brazilian security and intelligence authorities until one can fully judge the Brazilian and German commitment to privacy. On the whole, the domestic measures taken by liberal states cannot be seen as primarily targeted to changing the incentives for rule-consistent behavior.

However, theoretically stronger actions by liberal states could have been taken in order to advocate privacy. There are two reasons why this did not occur. First, there is a lack of concepts and rules for privacy as well as for behavior in cyberspace. There is no clear concept of privacy and no clear measures to successfully fight terrorism. Thus, it would be difficult to determine in which case possible sanctions should be lifted (Kietz 2013: 6), and that impedes coordinated and united actions of liberal states against the USA. Furthermore, a big part of the revealed mass surveillance practices (particularly the PRISM program) are not far away from what other countries do: They are also in control of their domestic communication system and demand that telephone and internet providers to develop their collection techniques in a way that is accessible for the government and to deliver information in cases of national security threats (Krieger 2014: 345). However, they do not store it and access this source only for targeted surveillance

75 The effort of states to prevent communications from travelling through the USA could lead to a so-called *balkanization*, which means a regionalization of the Internet. As some scholars hold (e.g. Gill 2015: 79f.), this development is unlikely because of the high social and economic costs.

practices. Last but not least, there is no regime for the governance of cyberspace. For a big part, the states' behavior in cyberspace is driven by anarchism until today (Gill 2015: 78).

Second, almost all liberal states cooperate with USA intelligence services. With the existence of the SIGINT alliance *Five Eyes,* Australia, Canada, New Zealand and the UK are automatically norm violators as well. Beyond that, other liberal states' intelligence services – e.g., of France and Germany – also have close relationships with the NSA (Smale 2015). The main problem is that this cooperation is not on equal footing. No Western intelligence service exists that does not rely on the NSA. Hence, a big power asymmetry drives the relationship between the NSA and other liberal states' intelligence services. To make matters worse, all states are in competition with each other for the best relationship to the NSA (Kietz 2013: 6 f.; Krieger 2014: 345 f.). Hence, the credibility of possible advocacy activities of liberal states is weakened enormously. That influences both the use of sanctions and discursive measures.

Persuasive and discursive measures are not fully available to liberal states' network either. Although the statements of liberal state leaders – particularly those from Rousseff – are the first step of persuasive measure by declaring the US behavior as norm violating and countering the mass surveillance practices with arguments (the universality of human rights), no long-term process of discussion has set in. This is due to the very heterogeneous understanding of privacy. To enter a long-term discussion with the norm violator USA, the community of advocating liberal states would need a definition of privacy that is shared by all of the actors. Moreover, the aforementioned weak credibility, which is caused by the norm violation of many liberal states, undermines possible persuasive measures. Unsurprisingly, Rousseff called for a multi-stakeholder approach to resolve the problem. It is, by the way, remarkable that most of the criticism of liberal states covered the surveillance of foreigners instead of criticizing the violation of privacy rights of American citizens in the same way.

All things considered, the liberal states have failed to set in motion any mode of social action in a comprehensive way. Although it has turned out that they prefer the mode of persuasion and discourse to react to the norm violation of the USA, they are not able to use this method effectively. For this reason, it seems that they rely on IOs to solve this problem because IOs seem more capable of doing so.

5.2. International Organizations

As aforementioned, the liberal states put much effort in activating IOs – particularly the UN – to react to the norm violation by the USA. Nevertheless, IOs are also by themselves strong advocates of human rights laws. In this section, the reaction of three IOs will be addressed: the UN, the EU, and the CoE.

5.2.1. United Nations

The only mode of social action that is possible at the UN-level is the one of persuasion and discourse. For coercive measures or the raising of sanctions, a resolution of the UN Security Council would be necessary. Because the USA holds a right of veto in this body, it is not possible for the UN member states to use coercive measures against the USA without their consent. Discursive measures, hence, are the only way for the UN to go.

In December 2013, the UN General Assembly (2013) adopted resolution 68/167 initiated by Brazil and Germany. The resolution recognized the right to privacy as set out in the UDHR and the ICCPR and

> 1. Reaffirms the right to privacy [...] and the right to the protection of the law against such interference [...];
> 2. Recognizes the global and open nature of the Internet [...];
> 3. Affirms that the same rights that people have offline must also be protected online, including the right to privacy;
> 4. Calls upon States: (a) To respect and protect the right to privacy, including in the context of digital communication; (b) To take measures to put an end to violations of those rights [...]; (c) To review their procedures [...] including mass surveillance, interception and collection, with a view to upholding the right to privacy by ensuring the full and effective

> implementation of all their obligations under international human rights law [...]. (United Nations General Assembly 2013)

Furthermore, the resolution asked the UN High Commissioner for Human Rights to provide a report on the protection of the right to privacy in relation to the surveillance practices of states. Half a year later, in June 2014, this report – which is called the "yardstick against surveillance" (Nyst/Falchetta 2017: 108) by privacy activists – was issued. In his report, the Commissioner clearly argues that the current surveillance practices by some states violate the right to privacy. Albeit the report agrees to the argument that electronic surveillance can be a "necessary and effective measure for legitimate law enforcement or intelligent purposes," it stresses that "compliance with article 17 of the International Covenant on Civil and Political Rights required that the integrity and confidentiality of correspondence should be guaranteed de jure and de facto" (United Nations Human Rights Council 2014 a: 6). Thereby, the report objects to the mass surveillance practices conducted by the USA and their allies, similar to the UN resolution. But the report goes further by actively contradicting arguments that are made to justify mass surveillance practices.

> [...] it has been suggested that the interception or collection of data about a communication, as opposed to the content of the communication, does not on its own constitute an interference with privacy. From the perspective of the right to privacy, this distinction is not persuasive. The aggregation of information commonly referred to as 'metadata' may give an insight into an individual's behaviour, social relationships, private preferences and identity that go beyond even that conveyed by accessing the content of a private communication. [...] It follows that any capture of communications data is potentially an interference with privacy and, further, that the collection and retention of communications data amounts to an interference with privacy [...]. (United Nations Human Rights Council 2014 a: 6 f.)

Moreover, the report objects to the argument often made by non-complying states that the conducted interferences of communications were in conformity with domestic law. "[...] interference that is permissible under national law may nonetheless be 'unlawful' if that national law is in conflict with the provisions of the International Covenant on Civil and Political Rights" (United Nations Human Rights Coucil 2014 a: 7). In view of the contribution of such surveillance programs to national security purposes the report states that the "degree of interference must, however, be assessed against the necessity of the measure to achieve that aim and the actual benefit it yields towards such a purpose" (United Nations Human Rights Coucil 2014a: 8). This would imply "that any communications surveillance programme must be conducted on the basis of a publicly accessible law, which in turn must comply with the State's own constitutional regime and international human rights law" (United Nations Human Rights Coucil 2014a: 10).

Last but not least, the UN High Commissioner on Human Rights criticises the argument that extraterritorial surveillance were automatically lawful, which also led to intelligence cooperation and the circumvention of domestic law by countries spying on each other's citizens.

> The Human Rights Committee, in its general comment No. 31, affirmed that States parties are required by article 2, paragraph 1, to respect and to ensure the Covenant rights to all persons who may be within their territory and to all persons subject to their jurisdiction. This means that a State party must respect and ensure the rights laid down in the Covenant to anyone within the power or effective control of that State Party, even if not situated within the territory of the State Party. This extends to persons within their 'authority.'
> The Human Rights Committee has been guided by the principle, as expressed even in its earliest jurisprudence, that a State may not avoid its international human rights obligations by taking action outside its territory that it would be prohibited from taking 'at home'. […] A State cannot avoid its human rights responsibilities simply by refraining from bringing those powers within the bounds of law. To conclude otherwise would not only undermine the universality and essence of the rights protected by international human rights law, but may also create structural incentives for States to outsource surveillance to each other.
> It follows that digital surveillance therefore may engage a State's human rights obligations if that surveillance involves the State's exercise of power or effective control in relation to digital communications infrastructure […]. Equally, where the State exercises regulatory jurisdiction over a third party that physically controls the data, that State also would have obligations under the Covenant. (United Nations Human Rights Council 2014a: 10ff.)

In March 2014, the HRC raised objections concerning the mass surveillance practices of the USA. In a country report on the USA, the HRC invites the state to "[t]ake all necessary measures to ensure that its surveillance activities, both within and outside the United States, conform to its obligations under the Covenant, including article 17" (UN HRC 2014 b: 10). The report shows particular concern about the weak possibilities of protection and remedy in cases of abuse of surveillance power. Although the USA did not ratify the procedure for individual complaints contained in the Optional Protocol, they ratified the IPCCR and so agreed to comply with it (United Nations Human Rights Council 2014 b; Pöschl 2015: 439 f.).

But this was not the only response by the UN to the Snowden revelations. It was recognized that the problem was also about the definition of privacy. Thus, a long-running process of discussion has been started. The members of the HRC agreed in March 2015 to establish a UN Special Rapporteur on Privacy (SRP). In August 2015, Joseph Cannataci was appointed as the UN's first SRP. He delivered his first annual report in March 2016 (United Nations Human Rights Council 2016: 3).[76]

The report serves mainly as a description of the mandate and how the SRP sees his task. According to the report, "the focus of the SRP shall be on informational privacy" (United Nations Human Rights Council 2016: 10). Of particular interest is the following statement, because it contradicts the argument of balancing security and liberty:

76 Before this, mass surveillance practices and the right to privacy were also addressed by a report of the Special Rapporteur on countering terrorism in 2014. It states that *certain states* violate international human rights law with their intelligence conduct: "State's obligations under article 17 of the International Covenant on Civil and Political Rights include the obligation to respect the privacy and security of digital communications. This implies in principle that individuals have the right to share information and ideas with one another without interference by the State, secure in the knowledge that their communication will reach and be read by the intended recipients alone. Measures that interfere with this right must be authorized by domestic law that is accessible and precise and that conforms with the requirements of the Covenant. They must also pursue a legitimate aim and meet the test of necessity and proportionality. [...] the technical reach of the programmes currently in operation is so wide that they could be compatible with article 17 of the Covenant only if relevant States are in a position to justify as proportionate the systematic interference with the Internet privacy rights of a potentially unlimited number of innocent people located in any part of the world. [...] there is an urgent need for States using this technology to revise and update national legislation to ensure consistency with international human rights law" (UN General Assembly 2014: 22).

> [I]t becomes clear that it is not only privacy that impacts the flows of information in society but also other rights like freedom of expression and freedom of access to publicly-held information. All of these rights are important and commitment to one right should not detract from the importance and protection of another right. Taking rights in conjunction wherever possible is healthier than taking rights in opposition to each other. Thus, properly speaking, it is not helpful to talk of 'privacy vs. security' but rather of 'privacy and security' since both privacy and security are desiderata … and both can be taken to be enabling rights rather than ends in themselves. Security is an enabling right for the overarching right to life while privacy may also be viewed as an enabling right in the overall complex web of information flows in society which are fundamentally important to the value of autonomy and the ability of the individual to identify and choose between options in an informed manner as he or she develops his or her own personality throughout life. (United Nations Human Rights Council 2016: 10)

That statement reveals the actual task of this discussion process: to address the basic argument of the proponents of mass surveillance and to challenge this point of view with a *better* argument – following the discourse theory of Habermas. This process of discussion will go on for the next few years. At the time of writing, the outcome can hardly be anticipated.

In August 2016, the second report of the SRP was published. The paper gives a description of the work progress. According to the report, the upcoming reports should highlight the right to privacy in five different focuses of activity called *Thematic Action Streams:* a better understanding of privacy; security and surveillance; big data and open data; health data; personal data held by cooperation (United Nations General Assembly 2016). With this report, the fields of discussion for the next years are defined.

Right down the line, the tactics of persuasion and discourse are the only ones used by the UN to face the violation of the human right to privacy. However, the UN uses this mode, based on the logic of appropriateness, in a very comprehensive way contrary to the single actions of many liberal states. This process of discussion follows three steps: In the first, the UN upholds the norm of privacy with a resolution to show that the behavior of the USA is not compliant with this norm. Second, they countered the arguments of the proponents of mass surveillance, who hold that the intelligence procedures of the USA and their allies are lawful and, hence, in accordance with the norm of privacy. And third, the UN launched a long-term discussion process aiming to challenge the underlying norm of mass surveillance as such. This does not mean that the UN would try to *destroy* this norm with counterarguments. Rather, the interpretation of the norm of security should no longer encounter the norm of privacy, so both can coexist.

Anyway, one has to keep in mind that besides the UN efforts since 2013 there is neither a new international law on privacy nor a new interpretation of the right to privacy (Peters 2017: 148 f.). Instead, the UN highly neglected the right to privacy, especially between 1989 and 2009 (Nyst/Falchetta 2017: 105).

5.2.2. European Union

According to Elmar Brok, the former chairman of the Foreign Affairs Committee at the EP, the mass surveillance practices of the USA caused an "enormous loss of trust" (2013, cited in Wright & Kreisl 2015: 11 f.). But from the three adequate modes of social action in this case (coercion, incentives, persuasion), only discursive measures were used to push the USA to a state of rule-consistent behavior. The EP proved to be the "most active European institution on the issues implicated by the NSA-Affair" (Schneider 2017: 557) in comparison to the Council and the Commission.

Although the EU could have raised sanctions against the USA, this was not possible because of the involvement of a considerable number of member states in mass surveillance practices. The Snowden revelations brought to light that not only the intelligence community *Five Eyes* exists, but other forms of cooperation like the *Nine Eyes* and the *14 Eyes* as well. These alliances are more limited forms of cooperation than the *Five Eyes,* a group of which the United Kingdom is a member. The club of the *Nine Eyes* includes the members of the *Five Eyes* as well as Denmark, France, the Netherlands and, as a non-EU member state, Norway. The group of the *14 Eyes* consists of the *Nine Eyes* and Belgium,

Germany, Italy, Spain and Sweden (Shane 2013). Because of these linkages to the NSA, the credibility of the EU member states to take measures to enforce the right to privacy is weak. Hence, it is unsurprising that the EP gave the strongest response to the NSA scandal and not the Council.

In July 2013, the EP adopted a Resolution *on the US National Security Agency surveillance programme, surveillance bodies in various Member States and their impact on EU citizens' privacy* that expressed

> 1. […] serious concern over PRISM and other such programmes, since, should the information available up to now be confirmed, they may entail a serious violation of the fundamental right of EU citizens and residents to privacy and data protection. […]
> 13. Stresses that in democratic and open states based on the rule of law, citizens have a right to know about serious violations of their fundamental rights and to denounce them, including those involving their own government; stresses the need for procedures allowing whistleblowers to unveil serious violations of fundamental rights and the need to provide such people with the necessary protection, including at international level […]. (European Parliament 2013)

Furthermore, the resolution requests that the USA provide all necessary information about surveillance practices and that they answer a letter by Commissioner Reding, sent only a few days after the first Snowden revelations to US Attorney General Holder, which demanded explanations from the US side. The Commission, moreover, should make sure that the standards of EU data protection would not be undermined in the negotiations about the Transatlantic Trade and Investment Partnership (TTIP). The resolution also calls on the Commission to review the Save Harbor agreement (European Parliament 2013).

On a final note, the EP instructed the Committee on Civil Liberties, Justice and Home Affairs (LIBE) to conduct an inquiry into today's surveillance practices and possible legal reforms. Committee members traveled to Washington and discussed with various officials and experts the US surveillance practices and held more than a dozen hearings in Brussels. At the end of this process, the EP adopted the LIBE report together with a resolution that expressed the main results of the report and demanded actions on behalf of these findings. Both the report and the resolution were passed in March 2014 and adopted by a large majority (Wright & Kreissl 2015: 12; European Parliament 2014).

In the resolution the EP considers the existence of far-reaching surveillance programs that were set in place by some states, pointing especially to the USA's PRISM program. They called the EU member states to revise their intelligence policy and existent oversight measures to comply with the right to privacy. But contrary to the first resolution, the EP did not only determine that a norm was violated, it also contradicted the arguments brought forward by supporters of mass surveillance practices. It

> 5. Notes that several governments claim that these mass surveillance programmes are necessary to combat terrorism; strongly denounces terrorism, but strongly believes that the fight against terrorism can never be a justification for untargeted, secret, or even illegal mass surveillance programmes; takes the view that such programmes are incompatible with the principles of necessity and proportionality in a democratic society [...];
> 10. Condemns the vast and systemic blanket collection of the personal data of innocent people, often including intimate personal information; emphasises that the systems of indiscriminate mass surveillance by intelligence services constitute a serious interference with the fundamental rights of citizens [...]. (European Parliament 2014)

By this, the EP contradicts the national security norm that justified surveillance practices. But does the EP's resolution also attack this norm in the same way as it was done by the UN? As it can be considered in the following quotation, the EP does not question the metaphor of the balance between security and privacy. Instead, the members of parliament call for states to strike the right balance between these norms. Nevertheless, they contradict the norm of security in the way that the EP denies that it is the only norm that applies to the practice of surveillance practices. The resolution

> 6. Recalls the EU's firm belief in the need to strike the right balance between security measures and the protection of civil liberties and fundamental rights, while ensuring the utmost respect for privacy and data protection; [...]
> 12. Sees the surveillance programmes as yet another step towards the establishment of a fully-fledged preventive state, changing the established paradigm of criminal law in democratic societies whereby any interference with suspects' fundamental rights has to be authorised by a judge or

> prosecutor on the basis of a reasonable suspicion and must be regulated by law; […]
> 16. Strongly rejects the notion that all issues related to mass surveillance programmes are purely a matter of national security and therefore the sole competence of Member States; reiterates that Member States must fully respect EU law and the ECHR while acting to ensure their national security […]. (European Parliament 2014)

But the EP did not only apply discursive measures to challenge the US' behavior, the resolution also demands "strong political undertakings from the new Commission which will be designated after the May 2014 European elections," (EP 2014) particularly regarding the adoption of a renewed data protection regime and the changes of the US Safe Harbor agreement.

The Safe Harbor agreement came to operation in 2000. With it, the Commission certified that the US data protection regime was congruent with the EU data protection laws. On the other hand, US companies that process data of EU citizens had to self-certify annually (in cooperation with the US Department of Commerce) that they abide by these rules (Wright & Kreissl 2015: 16). In light of the US surveillance practices, the EP demanded the suspension of this agreement from the Commission, because the members of parliament viewed the agreement as insufficient to protect the EU citizens' rights. The resolution notices that the Commission failed to act, although the same demand was already made in the 2013 EPs resolution (EP 2014). Nevertheless, in the very end it was not the Commission but the European Court of Justice that brought down the Safe Harbor agreement in 2015 (Gibbs 2015). Therefore, the Commission and US officials started negotiations about a new agreement that fits the EU law. In February 2016, the so-called *EU-US privacy shield* was launched. Basically, this shield consists of an annual written guarantee of the USA that their intelligence agencies have no indiscriminate access to the EU citizens data (Scott 2016). Although a working group in which every member state is represented criticized the privacy shield in April (Gibbs 2016), the privacy shield was published in the official gazette in August 2016. Only six weeks later, an Irish civil society organization took legal action against this privacy law at the European Court of Justice (Rudl 2016). Only a few days after taking office in January 2017, the 45th President of the United States, Donald Trump, issued an executive order that minimized the privacy rights of non-US citizens. At the time of writing, it is still unclear what consequences this will have for the validity of the privacy shield (Rebinger 2017).

With regard to the new Data Protection Regulation, changes were made after the Snowden revelations. One year before the NSA scandal, the USA successfully lobbied away a paragraph that demanded not to recognize any kind of judgment or decision of a court or an administration authority that requires disclosing personal data of a EU citizen. That would mean that the EU would not accept FISC warrants. But after the Snowden revelations, the entire paragraph was replaced word for word (Wright & Kreissl 2015: 16). When the new regulation was officially adopted in April 2016, however, the aforementioned paragraph was not included (EU 2016). Nevertheless, in Article 36.2 a it says that the Commission should decide about the adequacy of a third country's data protection standard with regard to the "rule of law, respect for human rights and fundamental freedoms, relevant legislation, both general and sectoral, including concerning public security, defense, national security and criminal law and the access of public authorities to personal data" (EU 2016).

After the revelation of the Snowden documents, some EU policy makers attempted to put on hold the negotiations concerning the TTIP (Wright & Kreissl 2015: 24).

Besides this, there was also a broader process of discussion that was launched. In early December 2015, the European Data Protection Supervisor (EDPS) established an Ethics Advisory Group that should start a broader discussion on EU level and globally about "how to ensure the integrity of our values while embracing the benefits of new technologies" (European Data Protection Supervisor 2016) and to explore "the relationships between human rights, technology, markets and business models in the 21st century from an ethical perspective, with particular attention to the implications for the rights to privacy and data protection in the digital environment" (European Data Protection Supervisor n.d.). The discussion should involve civil society actors as well as scientists and politicians.

In comparison to the EP, the Commission's and Council's reactions were considerably weak. The Commission, for example, did not initiate negotiations about a new privacy regime between the USA and the EU.

Instead, the Council of Justice of the European Union overturned the Safe Harbor agreement in the Schrems case (Schneider 2017: 540ff., 562). Also the European Council has been very reluctant in its response to the Snowden revelations (Schneider 2017: 562).

Summarizing the EU responses, one can observe that persuasive measures made up the largest part of it. The EU response followed to a certain degree the UN response: After discerning the norm violations, arguments against the violating behavior were made and – in the last step – a broader discussion process was initiated to discuss the relationship between privacy and modern techniques. Even attempts to negotiate new data protection arrangements with the USA have to be considered as persuasive measures. After all, the USA have to agree to such new agreements. Nonetheless, if the US continues to deny EU citizens sufficient data protection, the EU could sanction this with a refusal of a new Safe Harbor agreement. But because of the importance of a free flow of data between both the US and EU territories, it seems unlikely that this will happen.

5.2.3. Council of Europe

As early as 2008, the Commissioner of Human Rights of the CoE (CHR) noticed in his Issue Paper on *Protecting the Right to Privacy in the Fight Against Terrorism*: "We are rapidly becoming a 'Surveillance Society.' […] Freedom is being given up without gaining security" (13). Thus, it comes as no surprise that the Snowden revelations caused an ongoing response by the CHR. In further Issue Papers, he continued to challenge the security norm by arguing that the reasoning of national security was not an acceptable tool to minimize the validity of human rights (Commissioner of Human Rights 2015: 21ff.; Commissioner of Human Rights 2014: 107ff.). By publishing articles in several newspapers, the CHR reminded readers of the values of the European convention of human rights and expressed that untargeted mass surveillance could undermine the trust of citizens in the state and democratic values. He calls for the limitation of surveillance practices by law and a strong oversight of intelligence services (Muižnieks 2015; Muižnieks 2013). But did the Council of Ministers and the Parliamentary Assembly echo the efforts of the CHR?

The Snowden revelations definitely raised an awareness of the challenges to the right to privacy by technical developments. The CoE set in an Ad Hoc Committee on Data Protection (CAHDATA), which has the task to review and renew the Convention 108 on Data Protection, which played a major role in the development of data protection at the international level (Council of Europe n.d.b). At time of writing, results are still to be expected. Nevertheless, this was not the only response given by the CoE.

Only a few days after the first revelations were published by the *Guardian,* the Council of Ministers adopted a declaration acknowledging the threat of mass surveillance to the right to privacy, the right to free expression as well as to free media and reminding all member states that law enforcement activities have to comply with the CoE's human rights standards (Council of Europe 2013 a). A few months later, in November 2013, a second declaration was adopted by the member state's ministers for media and information society, which calls for safeguards against electronic mass surveillance. The declaration considers the destruction of democracy as possible and condemns the unlawful monitoring of communications (Council of Euorpe 2013 b).

The Parliamentary Assembly also adopted a resolution on mass surveillance in April 2015. It states that mass surveillance endangers human rights and calls for surveillance activities that are targeted and based on a court warrant and encourages national parliaments to carry out inquiries into the NSA affair (Council of Europe 2015 a). Additionally, it is notable that the resolution states "that, according to independent reviews carried out in the United States, mass surveillance does not appear to have contributed to the prevention of terrorist attacks, contrary to earlier assertions made by senior intelligence officials" (Council of Europe 2015 a). Another resolution, which was adopted in June 2015, called for a better protection of whistleblowers and asked the USA to let Snowden return to his home country and to give up the investigation against him for reasons of public interest (Council of Europe 2015 b).

In April 2016, the Council of Ministers adopted a recommendation encouraging states to evaluate their level of Internet freedom and Internet human rights standard periodically and share their findings with the CoE (Council of Europe 2016 a). To tackle the issue of human rights, rule of law and democracy in an online environment in the long run, the Council also adopted a New Internet Governance strategy in 2016 to launch a broad process of discussion. This includes specific steps and activities that should be accomplished by 2019. Among other things, a platform should be established where governments and Internet companies can launch a process of discussion about human rights online. In general, new standards regarding the behavior of Internet intermediaries should be established. To reach this target, the CoE wants to include governments, companies, civil society actors and academia in this discussion. As one of the key stakeholders, the UN-led Internet Governance Forum is mentioned. Particularly with regard to mass surveillance and the right to privacy, the Internet Governance strategy provides the international promotion of the CoE Convention 108 and triennial reports on the state of data protection in the member states on the basis of the renewed Convention 108 (Council of Europe 2016b).

In total, the responses of the CoE were only persuasive ones. This comes as no surprise, because the USA is not a member of the CoE. Hence, the coercive measure to sue the USA at the European Court of Human Rights was not available – contrarily to European accomplices of the USA.[77] The persuasive measures were directed at both the USA and the member states of the CoE. This makes sense considering the fact that at least 25 European security services or their governments, respectively, have cooperated with the USA in mass surveillance practices (Commissioner of Human Rights 2015: 20). Thus, in the first place, the reaction was not directed purely against the USA. Instead, member states were reminded that privacy is a precious human right.

77 E.g., Big Brother Watch et al. vs. United Kingdom. Generally, the United Kingdom is – as one of the closest partners of the USA in SIGINT – under peculiar scrutiny of the CHR, as a memorandum on surveillance in the UK shows (Commissioner of Human Rights 2016).

The internal persuasive measures, however, were recognized by the USA because of their observer status at the CoE (Commissioner of Human Rights n.d.c).

All in all, the persuasive measures of the CoE have the same structure as the responses of the UN and the EU. After objecting to the practices of the US and their allies, the norm that justified these measures was challenged with counterarguments (here: democratic values and research that shows that mass surveillance is not helpful to fight terrorism) leading to a broad multi-stakeholder discussion process about the right to privacy and other human rights in the digital age. As the next part of this chapter exhibits, the response of the (I)NGOs is similar to this.

5.3. (International) Non-Governmental Organizations: Amnesty International

The Snowden revelations caused a response by many international and domestic NGOs. Mainly, they used two modes of social actions to enhance the human right to privacy: coercion and persuasion. Even before the Snowden revelations many (I)NGOs advocated the right to privacy. The most far-reaching point of these activities was the development of the Necessary and Proportionate Principles, a soft law standard that should help to apply human rights to the technical world (Nyst/Falchetta 2017: 107). Nevertheless, also for the (I)NGOs the Snowden revelations can be seen as a starting point for a new phase of enhanced activity regarding the advocacy of the right to privacy.

The (I)NGOs informed the public about the norm violation in the Internet and with brochures. With it, they tried to cause awareness of this norm violation and create a public climate that is hostile to the government's norm violation. Thereby, they created pressure that could force the state to change its behavior. Protests were raised in Washington, D.C., and elsewhere in the world (Newell 2013), and even new NGOs originated through the Snowden revelations (Restore the Fourth 2015). However, aside from that, the NGOs also used the mode of legal enforcement to make the USA comply with human rights standards – at least to the extent that was still possible. As already mentioned in chapter four, the FAA cut the possibility of suing by exempting companies that acted on behalf of the government from being prosecuted. Many charges were brought against the surveillance activities conducted by the USA (American Civil Liberties Union n.d.; Electronic Frontier Foundation n.d.c); however, one was the most well-known one: ACLU vs. Clapper. The ACLU brought the claim against the mass collection of phone records of Americans to court only six days after the first revelations by the *Guardian*. The complaint argued that the NSA's surveillance program PSP violated the privacy rights of Americans protected by the Fourth Amendment. In May 2015, the Court of Appeals for the Second Circuit declared the program illegal (American Civil Liberties Union 2015). This case is considered to be the first successful outcome against the US surveillance activities.

As a matter of course, not all activities of all international and national NGOs can be considered in this chapter. But one organization should be scrutinized further: Amnesty International. One advantage of the investigation of AI is that it is one of the biggest human rights organizations on the globe and that the advocacy actions with regard to the right to privacy can be seen in comparison to advocacy processes of other human rights. In the following, the reactions of AI to the Snowden revelations will be analyzed.

Not only since the Snowden revelations AI was aware of the possible threat that the American law provided to human rights by granting huge possibilities of legal spying. Only a few months before the NSA affair had gone viral, the Supreme Court decided in Clapper vs. Amnesty International that AI was not allowed to challenge the existing surveillance laws allowing the security branch to intercept international communications of US persons because they cannot prove that they had been spied on (Liptak 2013). Hence, it is not remarkable that the organization strengthened their efforts to fight mass surveillance.

One of the first actions taken by AI was to support bodies of the international human rights regime with information. For example, AI provided a written statement to the UN HRC to discuss US behavior (Amnesty International 2013).

Whereas privacy rights and surveillance issues have not played a role in the public campaigning of AI until 2013, this changed after the Snowden revelations. In March 2015, AI launched the campaign *#Unfollowme,* which was directed mainly at the surveillance practices of the USA but also of the UK and other governments – making it the main global AI campaign against mass surveillance. With it, the INGO not only argues that the mass surveillance practices of states are intruding in the private sphere massively, they also supported this argument with a global poll. 15,000 people in 13 countries were surveyed on behalf of AI about the interception, storage and analysis of Internet user data. The poll found a majority in all countries against the huge capabilities of governments to conduct mass surveillance (Amnesty International 2015 a). Moreover, the campaign encompassed a petition to President Barack Obama, urging him to end mass surveillance practices that violate the privacy right of Americans and people around the globe; and to amend Executive Order 12333 that serves – among other things – as legitimation of the spying activities (Amnesty International n.d.a). In June 2015, the Board Members of AI USA wrote a letter to President Obama to communicate their concerns about US mass surveillance activities and to express that AI as an international human rights organization relies on secure and confidential communications with employees and victims of human rights violations. The letter also demands the amendment of Executive Order 12333, similar to the petition (Amnesty International 2015 b).

Nevertheless, the campaign was mainly initiated to raise attention to the issue of mass surveillance and, thus, to enhance public awareness of the issue. This was done by interviews with whistleblowers like Edward Snowden or by publishing information about what countries are involved in the NSA scandal and which country is sharing data with US authorities (Beaumont 2015 a; Amnesty International n.d.b). This awareness was also strengthened by a report about the importance of encryption in March 2016. It is Amnesty's first official position on the importance of encryption to human rights.

However, this campaign is different from other AI campaigns. One month after *#Unfollowme* was launched, AI stated that many comments had reached the organization, saying that surveillance was necessary and that one who had nothing to hide had nothing to fear – a response unthinkable to happen with regard to human right violations like torture or freedom of expression. These reactions showed AI how strong the security norm had proliferated even within societies. AI reacted by explaining in detail why such a point of view was not congruent with human rights (Beaumont 2015 b).

AI also cooperated with other human rights organizations and advocators of privacy rights. The organization joined campaigns like *Reset the net* (Amnesty International et al. n.d.) and helped develop software against surveillance activities of governments (Amnesty International 2014). Furthermore, together with Privacy International it published a brochure two years after the NSA affair had broken out to summarize the revelations and the main responses to it (Amnesty International & Privacy International 2015).

However, the right to privacy is not promoted in the same way as other human rights in cases of violation. The analysis of the annual reports since 2013 draws a picture of how diverse the right to privacy is and that it does not only apply to the surveillance issue.

In all annual reports of AI, mass surveillance is not mentioned in the section that deals with human right violations of the USA. Also with regard to other countries, the right to privacy is only a minor issue. Whereas in the latest annual report (Amnesty International 2016) concerns about a limitation of the right to privacy in European countries were expressed and UN efforts to enhance this human right are welcomed in the regional overview about Europe and Central Asia, the right to privacy was mentioned with regard to the state of human rights in single countries for different reasons. Brazil was lauded due to their efforts to enhance privacy; Australia, New Zealand and the UK were criticized for the surveillance activities of their intelligence services. Also new surveillance laws as well as the state of Internet privacy in countries like China, India, Korea, the Netherlands and others, were condemned. This does not always happen in relation to the mass surveillance practices but also with regard to the freedom of expression. Looking to other countries, like Iran, Morocco and South Africa, the right to privacy was mentioned in relation to the free choice of sexual practices and habits (Amnesty International 2016 a; Amnesty International 2015 c).

It is noteworthy that privacy is mentioned in several different capacities: in combination with sexual habits, freedom of expression and security issues. A human right that is as diverse as the right to privacy is more difficult to advocate. This does not mean that AI did not advocate the right to privacy, as a statement by Salil Shetty (cited in Amnesty International 2016 b), the AI's Secretary General, shows that privacy was mentioned when the latest annual report was launched:

> The misguided reaction of many governments to national security threats has been the crushing of civil society, the right to privacy and the right to free speech; and outright attempts to make human rights dirty words, packaging them in opposition to national security, law and order and 'national values.'

Nevertheless, the problem of correctly addressing the surveillance topic is existent. Although the US section of AI approaches the issue under the broad topic of *Security and Human Rights*, the right to privacy is addressed in two subchapters: *Freedom of expression* and *mass surveillance*. Whereas the racial profiling of mass surveillance activities and especially the violation of privacy of Muslim citizens is addressed in the *freedom of expression* category, the *mass surveillance* chapter deals with the intrusion into the privacy of citizens and non-citizens in general (Amnesty International n.d.c).

In addition, the intensity of advocacy of the right to privacy is also lower than the advocacy efforts of other human rights. One example of this is the *Amnesty Journal*, a periodical that is published every two months by the German section of AI, which covers topics of human rights violations and successes in the fight for human rights. From the time of the Snowden revelations until the end of May 2016, only a handful of articles were published that match the search terms *Überwachung* (surveillance), *NSA* or *Snowden*. In comparison to other human rights violations, the surveillance topic is underrepresented. Torture, one of the *classical* violations of human rights norms, is much more present in the journal: The term *Folter* (torture) leads to almost

100 articles in the same period (Amnesty International n.d.d). There are also no brochures about privacy or surveillance issues available on the German web page of AI (Amnesty International n.d.e).

In summary it can be said that the advocacy process of the right to privacy is different from the advocacy processes of other human rights. First of all, the topic of mass surveillance is quite new to AI. It took almost two years to launch the first global AI campaign on mass surveillance. Nevertheless, there are also other reasons that may explain the underrepresentation of the surveillance topic in the actions by AI. With a view to the annual reports and the Internet presence of AI regarding the presentation of the right to privacy and the violation of it through mass surveillance, it becomes obvious that privacy is a term that does not only touch many areas of life but also many human rights. Although the term privacy is mainly connected with the fight against mass surveillance, privacy is also at stake when it comes to freedom of expression and sexual self-determination. Last but not least, one main problem is the low visibility of privacy violations, as already mentioned in chapter three. This became apparent when many people voiced opposition to the campaign of AI against mass surveillance. Furthermore, the violation of privacy rights is hardly customizable – a tool very often used by AI to call attention to human rights violations.

In total, two modes of social action were used to prevail upon the USA to comply with the privacy norm: legal force and coercion. Nevertheless, the example of AI showed that it is not a simple task to campaign for the right to privacy. As aforementioned, several aspects can weaken the persuasive response of human rights organizations. Modes of coercion were also restricted, but civil liberties organizations used what was left of legal remedies to react to the human rights violation.

By having analyzed the actions of privacy advocates, it became apparent that the international advocacy network was activated by the Snowden revelations. But is there a discursive opportunity to change the behavior of the USA? Polls show that in the months after the Snowden revelations the attitude to privacy rights changed in the USA. Whereas a few days after the first revelations people considered the

NSA surveillance measures as acceptable, a few months later people said that the measures intrude their privacy rights and, thus, opposed the NSA activities, although people would still opt for security instead of privacy in case of doubt (Wright & Kreissl 2015: 20 f.). A symbol of a shifting value for privacy can be observed in increasing encryption activities worldwide (Wright & Kreissl 2015: 34 f.). This is an indication that a discursive opportunity in favor of the privacy advocacy network exists. Nevertheless, because of the weakness of the advocacy process, it can be doubted if the USA will reach the rule-consistent behavior stage in the near future, as the next chapter shows by scrutinizing the US reaction.

6. The US Response: Does the Spiral Model Work?

More than four years after the first revelations of documents pilfered by Edward Snowden a first assessment of the US reactions to national and international upheaval following the disclosures is possible. This chapter will briefly analyze whether the US reactions follow *spiral A* and will define at which of the five steps the USA can be located at the time of writing. I will conclude with a prospect of how likely it is that the USA will reach rule-consistent behavior with regard to the privacy norm in the foreseeable future.

1) *Repression:* Since 2001 and 2007, respectively, critical US surveillance procedures are being carried out. Although it was an individual and not an NGO that gave rise to the NSA affair, the connection to an international advocacy network – that is a determent of the spiral framework – was given: Snowden copied NSA documents and took them abroad; moreover, he contacted international journalists in order to arouse attention to the human rights violation. This was necessary, because internal competent authorities did not echo Snowden's concerns. Instead, superiors attacked Snowden to attempt to mute his concerns (Risen 2013). The first article containing information from documents taken by Snowden was published in a foreign newspaper and accused the USA of storing metadata of US citizen's calls (Greenwald 2013 a).

Hence, in the first place, the Snowden revelations followed the spiral model: An advocator contacted members of the international advocacy network to make human rights violations public and to pressure the state to change its behavior.

2) *Denial:* The steps of repression and denial coincide and cannot be separated exactly, because the phase of denial began long before the

Snowden revelations. Many US practices in cyberspace were already known before the revelations (O'Connel 2012), and rumors about overreaching surveillance practices of US intelligence agencies caused the Director of National Intelligence, James Clapper, as well as the NSA director, General Keith Alexander, to lie before Congress in early 2012 and early 2013, respectively. Questioned about possible surveillance activities targeting US persons, both denied any such activity (Cate 2015: 30).

According to the spiral model, this denial should strengthen the efforts of the human rights advocates – this did indeed happened. Even though the motivation of Snowden to divulge the surveillance activities dates back to 2007 (Risen 2013), the wrong answer of Alexander to members of Congress was the straw that broke the camel's back. In one of his first mails to journalist Laura Poitras, Snowden called this a main motivation to come forward: "NSA director Keith Alexander lied to Congress, which I can prove" (2013, cited in Greenberg 2014). Thus, the denial of the surveillance practices by state officials caused even greater pressure by human right advocates.

After the NSA affair had broken out, the USA could no longer deny the truthfulness of the accusations. Nevertheless, they remained in the denial phase for a few months, although they did not deny the most controversial matters of the Snowden leaks: the bulk phone data collection and the existence of PRISM. Instead of denying the practices themselves, the US government denied that these activities could be considered as norm violations. The Obama administration maintained, on the one hand, that the US spying activities on US citizens were legal and transparent (Reilly 2013) and, on the other hand, that in terms of foreign surveillance, US obligations under human rights treaties do not apply beyond US borders including the ICCPR (Fidler 2015 b: 58). Especially the statement on the extraterritorial non-application of the human right to privacy is in line with the tradition of US exceptionalism regarding human rights issues.[78]

78 In fact, the argument that human rights obligations are not applying extraterritorially is not made for the first time by the USA. The US government began to express this point of view in 1995 and expanded its use under the Bush administration (Van Schaack 2014: 22ff.). With it, the USA contradicts the doctrinal consensus of the international human rights bodies and advocates that "States owe human rights

The US government also engaged in the suppression of the advocacy process. Politicians not only called for sanctions on any country that takes in Snowden (Zengerle 2013), but the US government also threatened allied states, like Germany, which were considering to grant Snowden asylum (Scheer 2015). Furthermore, the US forced down the airplane of Bolivia's President Evo Morales in Vienna after rumors circulated that Snowden could be on board (Gathmann 2013). Nevertheless, privacy and civil liberties groups were not sanctioned in the USA and could continue their work. Suppression on a broad front, thus, did not happen.

3) *Tactical concessions/prescriptive status:* One can observe a time span in which the USA moved from the denial status to the phase of tactical concessions. The Obama administration started to enter this phase in August 2013, when the message Obama was conveying changed. Before, he had held the opinion that spying on Americans by the NSA was legal and everything was transparent thanks to the FISC. But in August, President Obama admitted for the first time that citizens might have a reason to worry about the NSA program by stating: "I think there are legitimate concerns people have that technology's moving so quick that at some point does the technology outpace the laws" (cited in Shapiro 2013). Additionally, Obama established a Presidential review group that was tasked to find a way in which the technical collection capabilities of the USA could be combined with the values of privacy and civil liberties (Shapiro 2013). Furthermore, the Privacy and Civil Liberties Oversight Board (PCLOB) was activated, and it reviewed the intelligence practices. In two reports, it held that the do-

obligations to all individuals within the authority, power, and control of their agents or instrumentalities" (Van Schaack 2014: 22). As Van Schaack (2014) holds, "this firm stance confirms the United States as a persistent objector to any emerging customary norm" (23).
Nevertheless, the philosophical roots of this point of view are going deeper and go back to the very establishment of human rights norms in the 1940s when the USA advocated the UDHR only as a statement of aspiration, rather than an approach of binding law. In fact, US governments have held the point of view that nothing can trump US law, and they never expected human rights treaties to be a kind of law. This attitude is commonly known as *US exceptionalism* (Forsythe 2002: 975ff.).

mestic bulk data collection was unconstitutional, whereas the PRISM program was not illegal (Cate 2015: 28 f.).

The moment when the USA totally entered the tactical concessions phase was January 17, 2014. On this day, the Presidential Policy Directive 28 (PPD-28) became effective and granted foreigners the same privacy rights as Americans already had under Executive Order 12333 (The White House 2014). On the same day, President Obama announced the changes he had made to intelligence policy by this directive.

In his speech, President Obama maintained that he had always been skeptical about the surveillance capabilities of the NSA and that he had ordered some changes after taking office. Nevertheless, he did not stop the programs completely, because according to him, there was no evidence that the NSA was using these powers to violate the law. Obama nonetheless defended the necessity of these programs to prevent future attacks on America (Obama 2014: 321 f.). However, he agreed that the programs were never a subject of public discussion, although this is necessary in a democratic country.

> And for these reasons, I indicated in a speech at the National Defense University last May that we needed a more robust public discussion about the balance between security and liberty. […] the task before us now is greater than simply repairing the damage done to our operations or preventing more disclosures from taking place in the future. Instead, we have to make some important decisions about how to protect ourselves and sustain our leadership in the world, while upholding the civil liberties and privacy protections that our ideals and our Constitution require. (Obama 2014: 322)

This paragraph addressed the American people and the domestic surveillance activities of the NSA. Obama stuck to the balance metaphor of privacy and security. However, he accepted the norm of privacy without calling the NSA program a violation of this norm – a typical tactical concession in matters of discourse. And also with regard to the surveillance of foreigners, Obama acknowledged the norm of privacy, although he again upheld the balance metaphor.

> Our capabilities help protect not only our nation, but our friends and our allies, as well. But our efforts will only be effective if ordinary citizens in other countries have confidence that the United States respects their privacy, too. […] In other words, just as we balance security and privacy at

> home, our global leadership demands that we balance our security requirements against our need to maintain the trust and cooperation among people and leaders around the world. […] The bottom line is that people around the world, regardless of their nationality, should know that the United States is not spying on ordinary people who don't threaten our national security, and that we take their privacy concerns into account in our policies and procedures. This applies to foreign leaders as well. […] Now let me be clear: Our intelligence agencies will continue to gather information about the intentions of governments – as opposed to ordinary citizens – around the world, in the same way that the intelligence services of every other nation does. We will not apologize simply because our services may be more effective. (Obama 2014: 327 f.)

This paragraph also shows a typical tactical concession. Sensing that the legal arguments brought forward were not helping to get rid of the privacy advocators, President Obama, after denying that US behavior violated human right norms, now acknowledged reasonable privacy interests of foreign individuals.

However, this speech was not successful in satisfying the claims of privacy advocates but initiated further critiques – as the spiral model prescribes it. First of all, the Obama speech as well as PPD-28, is about *privacy interests* and *privacy concerns* that should be taken into account instead of *privacy rights*. Hence, the US government still does not accept privacy as an individual right held by every person vis-à-vis US intelligence services. Second, the concession made to privacy in both the speech and the directive apply only after the collection of information. The collection is not seen as an intrusion into privacy itself (Fidler 2015 b: 58). Unsurprisingly, PPD-28 was not sufficient enough to calm the critics.

At least at the domestic level, Obama took further steps. Two months after he had ordered PPD-28 and defended the bulk collection of phone data, the US government declared to no longer be collecting these data. Instead, the intelligence services would demand the data from the telecommunication companies on behalf of an individual FISC order. The legislation of Congress was needed to adopt this approach. It resulted in the USA Freedom Act, signed by President Obama in June 2015. Among other things, the bill cancelled Section 2015 of the USA Patriot Act and, thus, bulk collection of phone metadata was no longer allowed (Fidler 2015 a: 331; Cohn & Reitman 2015). On

November 28, 2015, the NSA bulk metadata collection ended officially (MacAskill 2015).

Although the USA Freedom Act restricted surveillance capabilities enormously, the law has to be considered as a further tactical concession. Neither did the act change the existence of Section 702 of the FAA, which is the determinant for the PRISM program that also affects the Internet privacy of US persons; nor was Executive Order 12333 amended, which is the legal basis for most of the international NSA surveillance activities (Cohn & Reitman 2015). Furthermore, if the Obama administration had not acted, it would have been forced to do so by the Supreme Court ruling ACLU vs. Clapper, which was issued in May 2015 and which declared the bulk metadata collection as incompatible with the Fourth Amendment rights of Americans. Hence, if no further laws will be enacted in the future, the Freedom Act can hardly be taken as a commitment to the human right to privacy, rather as a mere concession made to the advocacy network.

Other scholars may have a different view. As Johnson (2016) remarks, the PPD-28 "took the 'unprecedented' step of extending certain privacy protections afforded to U.S. persons to those overseas. [...] On the global scale, such an announcement was the first of its kind" (230). And Brown et al. (2017) consider the results of the NSA affair in the following way: Both PPD-28 and the USA Freedom Act contain "clearer rules and greater limits than the equivalent regime of almost all E.U. Member States. [...] In the absence of clear and specific rules in other countries, ironically the United States now serves as a baseline for foreign surveillance standards" (463). And Johnson (2016) seconds:

> [...] it is no surprise, that the language used in PPD-28 extending certain privacy protections to foreign nationals mirrors the language of the U.N. resolution. [...] Firmly placing electronic surveillance within the framework of international human rights law, it begins the discussion of what potential customs and legal restraint might look like, lessening the risk for continued growth of such programs without any serious consideration as to implications on individual rights. With the Obama Administration's issuance of PPD-28, America is now positioned to lead the debate. (245)

Reading such judgments, one may wonder why the USA are not considered as a state of rule-consistent behavior. But the classification of the USA as a new spearhead of the right to privacy in the digital age – as some of these utterances suggest – cannot hide the fact that the USA, like many European states, does not comply with the right to privacy in international law. Peters (2017) put it very simply: "Both privacy and the confidentiality of correspondence are protected by the Human Rights Covenant, even in the Internet. This means that the 2013 General Assembly Resolution does not articulate new law, not even a new interpretation of the law" (148 f.). Hence, even if the USA created with the PPD-28 and the Freedom Act more sophisticated privacy rights than those that are in place in European states, this does not automatically make them a rule-consisting state. And the fact that the Snowden revelations triggered an international debate about Internet privacy does not mean that privacy rights had not been valid in the digital world before 2013. The debate about digital privacy rights launched by the UN, (I)NGOs and some liberal states is undoubtedly necessary. But this necessity evolves from the bare fact that many states violated privacy rights in the digital world for years – and not from an alleged gap in the international law.

At least at the domestic level, the USA took further steps to ensure privacy rights of Americans, which partly pushed the USA to the level of *prescriptive status.* According to the original spiral model, this phase is the one in which the validity of human rights norms is accepted. This results in the ratification of relevant human rights treaties and the adoption of domestic human rights legislation. Moreover, a change should happen in discourse, expressed in the states' references to human rights norms in public and bureaucratic discourse (Risse et al. 2013). Of course, this definition has to be amended when it comes to the assessment of the behavior of a former rule-consistent state. This means that in the case of the USA, the US government never released the signature of the ICCPR or the UDHR. Nevertheless, prescriptive status can still be observed by enacting laws and orders to bring the behavior of the state in line with existing international human rights laws.

However, further laws are going to be adopted. In April 2016, the House of Representatives unanimously passed the E-mail Privacy Act. The Act would require the government to get a court warrant to access private communications and documents of US citizens stored online at

Internet companies (Cope 2016). This would be a step towards prescriptive status. But the bill did not pass the Senate in the 114th Congress and was reintroduced in the 115th Congress and passed the House of Representatives in February 2017. The Senate vote on the bill is remaining at the time of writing (Greenberg 2017).

At the international level, no further steps have been taken to achieve the prescriptive status – although PPD-28 was a very important milestone on this way. In the near future, this is unlikely to happen. Although this chapter has shown that the spiral model is applicable to former rule-consistent states and that the US behavior in the response to the Snowden revelations follows the approach by Risse et al., two things make it unlikely that the USA will reach the rule-consistent-behavior status with regard to the right to privacy in the near future: the scope conditions and a weak advocacy network. First of all, the USA as a hegemonic power are less materially vulnerable than other states (Sikkink 2013: 162). And even though the sensitivity to human rights norms rose with the inauguration of Obama as US President (Sikkink 2013: 162), the Obama administration has shown only a limited social vulnerability with regard to privacy at the international level. Last but not least, this social vulnerability is weakened by the behavior of other liberal states. As Muižnieks (2015) remarks, many European states facing recent terror attacks have toughened their security laws and weakened their privacy rights since the Snowden disclosures. This does not only weaken the response from liberal states themselves but also from many international human rights bodies like IOs.

Nevertheless, this chapter proved that the advocacy process has influenced the behavior of the USA. Moreover, it has been shown that the response follows the framework of the spiral model. After having analyzed the regress of the privacy norm as well as the reaction to the Snowden disclosures, the next chapter concludes the main findings.

7. Conclusion: Privacy – a Dead Norm?

The task of this paper was twofold: On the one hand, the norm regression of privacy (defined as communicational and informational privacy) in the USA should have been analyzed using the spiral model; on the other hand, the advocacy process as well as the US reaction to this regression should have been scrutinized.

With reference to the process of norm regress, this paper developed a theoretical approach that is able to explain the processes of both norm diffusion and norm regress at the domestic level. The comprehensive spiral model is capable of covering the dynamics, changing influences and normative arguments that influence the behavior of states as well as the advocacy process. Furthermore, the different stages could not only be defined by the usage of discursive means but also by legislative acts and actions of the state. Nevertheless, there is need for further research to find out what follows from a norm regression with regard to advocacy actors (like NGOs). One of the questions that have to be answered is if the norm regression goes hand in hand with the repression of advocators.

According to the comprehensive spiral model, the norm regression of privacy in the USA is at an advanced stage. The norm is not only encountered rhetorically but also by legal means. This goes so far that the right to privacy is officially diminished by law so it does not apply anymore to the international communications of US citizens. The complete abolishment of the right to privacy would be the next step. Nevertheless, the advocacy process was not unsuccessful. The case study of this paper has also shown that the struggle between human rights norms and the security norm is far older than one and a half decades. Not even since 9/11 a security norm has been developed.

Nevertheless, the comprehensive spiral model fails to explain developments at the international level. It can neither explain the diffusion of a counter-norm internationally, nor can it explain the state of regression of the privacy norm in the international arena. According to the comprehensive spiral model, the state of norm regression regarding privacy internationally would be 'circumvention,' because secret norm violations of many actors were discovered. Nevertheless, the norm of security already massively challenges the norm of privacy in public discourse, albeit no contracts or treaties have been altered that deal with the right to privacy.

One example is the UN *World Summit on the Information Society*, which was held in Geneva and Teheran in 2003 and 2005, respectively, and discussed Internet governance of the future. Although privacy and data protection have been matters of some debate, the summit was characterized by security concerns of states after terror attacks in the US and Europe. Through pressure by EU member states, privacy was mentioned in the final statement of the summit, but this was not enough to satisfy the bulk of the participating NGOs. In protest, the representatives of civil society published their own final statement, which was much more focused on privacy issues (Schiedermair 2012: 130ff.).

It would also be of interest to see, if the domestic norm regression in the USA caused a norm violation by the USA on the international level. It remains also unclear if the norm violation by the USA has inspired other states to violate the norm of privacy as well. As aforementioned, the case study on the USA as well as the comprehensive spiral model cannot answer these questions.

That should not hide the fact that questions regarding privacy and international surveillance activities were already raised by the EP in 2001 (Brown et al. 2017: 464). Law making in this field is highly needed (Peters 2017: 177). One has to acknowledge that the USA has taken substantial steps regarding the transparency of international surveillance. As Brown et al. (2017) mention, PPD-28 and the Freedom Act created "clearer rules and greater limits than the equivalent regime of almost all E.U. Member States. […] In the absence of clear and specific rules in other countries, ironically the United States now serves as a baseline for foreign surveillance standards" (463).

The comprehensive spiral model cannot explain developments in international surveillance and privacy standards. This is unsurprising, because the original spiral model was developed to explain domestic state behavior. For the international spread of counter-norms, other models may be more helpful to explain the norm change – one example may be Wiener's (2014) theory of contestation. Additionally, the comprehensive model is only capable of explaining the rise and fall of human right norms. Other norms that do not rely on the availability of an international advocacy network, including entrepreneurs like (I)NGOs and IOs, cannot be analyzed with the comprehensive spiral model. The theoretical framework is not able to explain the emergence of a human rights norm at the international level either.

Furthermore, the comprehensive spiral model was developed in view of weak and imprecise human rights. As recent publications indicate, there exists a difference in the process of norm regression between vague and precise norms (Panke & Petersohn 2016). Hence, further research has to be done on the applicability of the comprehensive spiral model to other human rights norms. It can be assumed that the regression of strong and precise norms develops differently. This is mainly because it will be more difficult to create an equilibrium between a precise human right (like the right to life or the prohibition of torture) and a counter norm. A tradeoff between a strong human right and a counter norm would possibly cause stronger protests in public and could be advocated more easily. As a result, such an equilibrium might not be established in law or treaties but merely by discursive means and in practice.

Nonetheless, this paper has shown that after the Snowden revelations a window of discursive opportunity existed and that a transnational advocacy network was activated. Although the activities of the advocacy network were not unsuccessful, several circumstances have prevailed to make the USA comply with the norm of privacy again.

First of all, the norm of privacy is a vague norm. As shown in the third chapter, the only common point of the multitude of privacy conceptions is the limited access to the self. How this is implemented in analog and digital life is a contentious issue. Although the European conception of privacy in the digital area (data protection) is dominant, there exists, especially in the USA, a different conception of the norm of privacy. Hence, certain measures to make the USA comply with the privacy norm – like sanctions – are useless, as long as there does not exist a common understanding concerning the definition of the violated norm and thus concerning the question when sanctions should be lifted. To make matters worse, privacy is a human rights norm that is difficult to advocate in public, because the absence of privacy does not cause harm directly. Thus, the distinctive feature of privacy is a main reason why the privacy entrepreneurs failed to make the USA comply with this norm.

Second, the multilateral and mutual norm violation minimizes the number of privacy advocates considerably. Especially with regard to liberal states, the norm violations disqualify these states as norm advocators because of a weakened public credibility. Only a few liberal states were able to condemn the surveillance practices of the USA resolutely. Because of the low credibility, liberal states were not even able to launch a discourse with the aim of convincing the USA of the correctness of the privacy norm in the long run. The use of other, stronger modes of social action, such as coercion or incentives, were not even imaginable.

Third, primarily discursive measures were used to react to the norm violating behavior of the USA because of the weak advocacy capability of the liberal states. This approach was mainly carried out by IOs and (I)NGOs. Albeit this is the social action that grants the most sustainable results (nothing is *better* than an actor that is deeply convinced of a human rights norm), it is also the weakest tool to react to norm violations.

Fourth, because the domestic norm regression is at an advanced stage, normative arguments in favor of privacy are countered by normative arguments in favor of the counter-norm of security. That the security norm resonates enormously, even in public, was shown to AI when a lot of people criticized their effort to advocate the right to privacy. But this also holds true for the USA: The more advanced the norm regress is, the weaker is the social vulnerability. This becomes clear with repect to the discursive use of the term privacy. Still, the USA did not officially speak of a *right* to privacy, merely privacy *interests* were mentioned. The counter discourse influenced even international norm advocates and made them adopt argumentative structures (like the balance metaphor) to defend the norm of privacy. Nevertheless, the USA was forced to acknowledge privacy as something humans deserve, even if they refuse to classify it as a right, and although the USA remains a powerful state with a low material vulnerability, which influences the effectiveness of certain social modes of action, like coercion or sanctions.

Although the death of the privacy norm is theoretically still possible in the USA at the domestic level (because the prescriptive status is not totally reached yet), it is not likely. The activation of the spiral model has influenced the behavior of the USA. Tactical concessions have been made, which implies a rhetorical acknowledgement of the norm. This alone does not guarantee the development of the USA toward rule-consistent behavior. Nevertheless, it is now hardly possible that the norm will die completely, because even the violator has acknowledged its existence.

Nevertheless, the discursive processes that followed the norm violation of the USA at the international level can also have a weakening effect to privacy. It is possible that other actors adopt the normative arguments of the encountering norm and that at the very end a compromise is created between privacy and security. This would be a further weakening of the norm of privacy at the international level.

According to some scholars, this would not come as a surprise. They predict the death of the norm of privacy, making the point that technological developments will necessarily lead to the abolishment of the privacy norm (Chesterman 2011: 4). While the challenge of privacy by new technologies is undoubted, it is at the end of the day not the technological development itself but counter-norms that lead to the possible abolishment of the privacy norm. Warren and Brandeis may turn in their graves then: Wasn't it precisely technological progress that made them create the right to privacy?

Bibliography

Abu-Laban, Yasmeen (2014): The politics of surveillance. Civil liberties, human rights and ethics, in: *Routledge Handbook of Surveillance Studies*, Kristie Ball et al. (eds.), Abingdon: Routledge, pp. 420–427.

Adler, David Gray (2008): George Bush, the unitary executive and the Constitution, in: *US National Security, Intelligence and Democracy. From Church Committee to the War on Terror*, Russell Miller (ed.), Abingdon: Routledge, pp. 99–119.

Agamben, Giorgio (2015): Die Geburt des Sicherheitsstaats, in: *Die Überwacher. Prism, Google, Whistleblower*, Edition Le Monde diplomatique No. 16, Dorothee d'Aprile (ed.), pp. 7–9.

Aid, Mattew (2009): *The Secret Sentry. The Untold History of the National Security Agency*, New York: Bloomsbury Press.

Aiken, Katherine (2008): Senator Church and his constituents, in: *US National Security, Intelligence and Democracy. From Church Committee to the War on Terror*, Russell Miller (ed.), Abingdon: Routledge, pp. 76–95.

Altmann, Irwin (1977): Privacy Regulation: Culturally Universal or Culturally Specific?, in: *Journal of Social Issues*, Vol. 33, No. 3, pp. 66–84.

American Civil Liberties Union (2015): *ACLU V. Clapper – Challenge to NSA Mass Call-Tracking Program*, available at: https://www.aclu.org/cases/aclu-v-clapper-challenge-nsa-mass-call-tracking-program [accessed: 05/25/2016].

American Civil Liberties Union (2001): *In Defence of Freedom in a Time of Crisis*, available at: https://www.aclu.org/defense-freedom-time-crisis [accessed: 04/19/16].

American Civil Liberties Union (n.d.): *Court battles*, available at: https://www.aclu.org/defending-our-rights/court-battles?topics=132 [accessed: 05/25/2016].

Amnesty International (2016 a): *Amnesty International Report 2015/16. The State of the World's Human Rights*, available at: https://www.amnesty.org/en/latest/research/2016/02/annual-report-201516/ [accessed: 05/25/2016].

Amnesty International (2016 b): *Amnesty International State of the World 2015–2016*, available at: http://www.amnestyusa.org/research/reports/amnesty-international-state-of-the-world-2015-2016?page=show [accessed: 05/25/2016].

Amnesty International (2015 a): *Global opposition to USA big brother mass surveillance*, 03/18/2015, available at: https://www.amnesty.org/en/latest/news/2015/03/global-opposition-to-usa-big-brother-mass-surveillance/ [accessed: 05/34/2016].

Amnesty International (2015 b): *Global Surveillance Operations and the Risk to Human Rights*, 06/06/2015, available at: http://www.amnestyusa.org/pdfs/AIUSA_GlobalSurveillanceBoardLetter_20150606.pdf [accessed: 05/24/2016].

Amnesty International (2015 c): *Amnesty International Report 2014/15. The State of the World's Human Rights*, available at: https://www.amnesty.org/en/latest/research/2016/02/annual-report-201516/ [accessed: 05/25/2016].

Amnesty International (2014): *New tool for spy victims to detect government surveillance*, 11/20/2014, available at: https://www.amnesty.org/en/latest/news/2014/11/new-tool-spy-victims-detect-government-surveillance/ [accessed: 05/24/2016].

Amnesty International (2013): *The US NSA and the UK GCHQ want to listen in on all: Time for the Human Rights Council to discuss their activities: Amnesty International written statement to the 24th session of the UN Human RightsCouncil (9 to 27 September 2013)*, 08/29/2013, AI index: IOR 41/018/2013.

Amnesty International (n.d.a): *Stand Up For Our Rights Online!*, available at: http://act.amnestyusa.org/ea-action/action?ea.client.id=1839&ea.campaign.id=36747 [accessed: 05/24/2016].

Amnesty International (n.d.b): *Does your country share your data with the USA?*, available at: https://www.amnesty.org/en/latest/campaigns/2015/06/does-your-country-share-your-data-with-the-usa/ [accessed: 05/24/2016].

Amnesty International (n.d.c): *Human Rights and National Security*, available at: http://www.amnestyusa.org/our-work/issues/security-and-human-rights [accessed: 05/25/2016].

Amnesty International (n.d.d): *Suchbegriffe*, available at: http://www.amnesty.de/suche?words-advanced=Folter&search.x=0&search.y=0&search=Suchen&country=&topic=&node_type=ai_journal_story&from_month=6&from_year=2013&to_month=4&to_year=2016&sort_type=desc&page_limit=10&form_id=ai_search_form#resultlist [accessed: 05/25/2016].

Amnesty International (n.d.e): *Broschüren*, available at: https://www.amnesty.de/2010/9/26/broschueren?destination=node%2F16659 [accessed: 05/25/2016]

Amnesty Internaional et al. (n.d.): *Reset the net*, available at: https://www.resetthenet.org [accessed: 05/24/2016].

Amnesty International/Privacy International (2015): *Two years after Snowden*, available at: https://www.amnesty.org/en/documents/act30/1795/2015/en/ [accessed: 05/25/2016].

Ashby, LeRoy (2008): The Church Committee's history and relevance. Reflecting on Senator Church, in: *US National Security, Intelligence and Democracy. From Church Committee to the War on Terror*, Russell Miller (ed.), Abingdon: Routledge, pp. 57–75.

Atkinson, L. Rush (2015): Regulating the Surveillance State, Upstream and Down: A Law & Economics Approach to the Intelligence Framework and Proposed Reforms, in: *Stanford Journal of International Law*, Vol. 51, No.1, pp. 1–18.

Bamford, James (2009): *The Shadow Factory. The Ultra-Secret NSA from 9/11 to the Eavesdropping on America*, New York: Anchor Books.

Beaumont, Ben (2015 a): *Edward Snowden: "I should have come forward sooner,"* 06/04/2015, available at: https://www.amnesty.org/en/latest/campaigns/2015/06/edward-snowden-i-should-have-come-forward-sooner/ [accessed: 05/24/2016].

Beaumont, Ben (2015 b): *7 reasons why 'I've got nothing to hide' is the wrong response to mass surveillance*, 04/29/2015, available at: https://www.amnesty.org/en/latest/campaigns/2015/04/7-reasons-why-ive-got-nothing-to-hide-is-the-wrong-response-to-mass-surveillance/ [accessed: 05/24/2016].

Beck, Ulrich (1986): *Risikogesellschaft. Auf dem Weg in eine andere Moderne*, Frankfurt a.M.: Suhrkamp

Bedan, Matt (2007): Echelon's Effect: The Obsolescence of the US Foreign Intelligence Legal Regime, in: *Federal Communications Law Journal*, Vol. 59, No. 2, pp. 425–444.

Bennett, Colin (2014): Privacy advocates, privacy advocacy and the surveillance society, in: *Routledge Handbook of Surveillance Studies*, Kristie Ball et al. (eds.), Abingdon: Routledge, pp. 412–419.

Bennett, Colin (2011): Storming the Barricades so We Can All Be Private Together: Everyday Surveillance and the Politics of Privacy Advocacy, in: *Sichtbarkeitsregime. Überwachung, Sicherheit und Privatheit im 21. Jahrhundert*, Leon Hempel et al. (eds.), Wiesbaden: Springer VS Verlag, pp. 299–320.

Bennett, Colin (1992): *Regulating Privacy. Data Protection and Public Policy in Europe and the United States*, Ithaca: Cornell University Press.

Biermann, Kai (2017 a): Was der NSA-Ausschuss erreicht hat und was nicht, in: *Zeit online*, 06/28/2017, available at: http://www.zeit.de/politik/deutschland/2017-06/ueberwachungsaffaere-nsa-untersuchungsausschuss-abschlussbericht-faq/komplettansicht [accessed: 09/05/2017].

Biermann, Kai (2017 b): Opposition wirft Regierung Lüge vor, in: *Zeit online*, 06/19/2017, available at: http://www.zeit.de/politik/deutschland/2017-06/nsa-untersuchungsausschuss-bnd-abschlussbericht-opposition [accessed: 09/05/2017].

Biermann, Kai (2017 c): Selbstherrliche Überwachung soll Gesetz werden, in: *Zeit online*, 06/07/2017, available at: http://www.zeit.de/politik/deutschland/2016-06/nsa-bnd-verfassungsschutz-ueberwachung-gesetz-entwurf/komplettansicht [accessed: 09/05/2017].

Blum, Stephanie Cooper (2009): What Really is at Stake with the FISA Amendments Act of 2008 and Ideas for Future Surveillance Reform, in: *Boston University Public Interest Law Journal*, Vol. 2, pp. 269–314.

Bogart, William (2014): Simulation and post-panopticism, in: *Routledge Handbook of Surveillance Studies*, Kristie Ball et al. (eds.), Abingdon: Routledge, pp. 30–37.

Boghosian, Heidi (2013): *Spying on Democracy. Government Surveillance, Corporate Power, and Public Resistance*, San Francisco: City Lights Books.

Brivot, Marion/Yves Gendron (2011): Beyond panopticism: On the ramifications of surveillance in a contemporary professional setting, in: *Accounting, Organizations and Society*, Vol. 36, No. 3, pp. 135–155.

Brown, Ian/Morton Halperin/Ben Hayes et al. (2017): Toward Multilateral Standards for Foreign Surveillance Reform, in: *Privacy and Power. A Transatlantic Dialogue in the Shadow of the NSA-Affair*, Russel Miller (ed.), Cambridge: Cambridge University Press, pp. 461–491.

Brown, Ian (2013): Anforderung an die Ermächtigung zur rechtmäßigen Abhörung, in: *Überwachtes Netz. Edward Snowden und der größte Überwachungsskandal der Geschichte*, Markus Beckedahl/Andre Meister (eds.), Berlin: newthinking communications, pp. 206–213.

Buckley, John (2014): *Managing Intelligence. A Guide to Law Enforcement Professionals*, Boca Raton: CRC Press.

Bunz, Mercedes: *Vom Speicher zum Verteiler. Die Geschichte des Internet*, Berlin: Kadmos.

Bygrave, Lee A. (2010): Privacy and Data Protection in an International Perspective, in: *Scandinavian Studies in Law*, Vol. 56, pp. 165–200.

Cate, Fred H. (2015): Edward Snowden and the NSA: Law, Policy, and Politics, in: *The Snowden Reader*, David Fidler (ed.), Bloomington: Indiana University Press, pp. 26–44.

Ceyhan, Ayse (2014): Surveillance as biopower, in: *Routledge Handbook of Surveillance Studies*, Kristie Ball et al. (eds.), Abingdon: Routledge, pp. 38–45.

Chaos Computer Club (n.d.): *Chaos Computer Club*, available at: https://www.ccc.de/en/home [accessed: 01/20/2016].

Chesterman, Simon (2011): *One Nation Under Surveillance. A New Social Contract to Defend Freedom Without Sacrificing Liberty*, Oxford: Oxford University Press.

Chinese National Ministry of Defense (2014): Statement on U.S. Indictment of Chinese Military Officers, in: *The Snowden Reader*, David Fidler (ed.), Bloomington: Indiana University Press, p. 165.

Christie, George (1972): Government Surveillance and Individual Freedom: A Proposed Statutory Response to Laird vs. Tatum and the Broader Problem of Government Surveillance of the Individual, in: *New York University Law Review*, Vol. 47, pp. 871–902.

Clarke, Roger (1988): Information Technology and Dataveillance, in: *Communications of the Association for Computing Machinery*, Vol. 31, No. 5, pp. 498–512.

Cohn, Cindy/Rainey Reitman (2015): *USA Freedom Act Passes: What We Celebrate, What We Mourn, and Where We Go From Here*, 06/02/2015, available at: https://www.eff.org/deeplinks/2015/05/usa-freedom-act-passes-what-we-celebrate-what-we-mourn-and-where-we-go-here [accessed: 05/29/2016].

Cole, David (2003): The new McCathyism: Repeating History in the War on Terrorism, in: *Harvard Civil Rights-Civil Liberties Law Journal*, Vol. 38, No. 1, pp. 1–30.

Commissioner of Human Rights (2016): *Memorandum on surveillance and oversight mechanisms in the United Kingdom*, 05/16/2016, available at: https://wcd.coe.int/com.instranet.InstraServlet?command=com.instranet.CmdBlobGet&InstranetImage=2919538&SecMode=1&DocId=2375752&Usage=2 [accessed: 05/23/2016].

Commissioner of Human Rights (2015): *Democratic and effective oversight of national security services*, available at: https://wcd.coe.int/com.instranet.InstraServlet?command=com.instranet.CmdBlobGet&InstranetImage=2796355&SecMode=1&DocId=2286978&Usage=2 [accessed: 05/23/2016].

Commissioner of Human Rights (2014): *The rule of law on the Internet and in the wider digital world*, available at: https://wcd.coe.int/com.instranet.InstraServlet?command=com.instranet.CmdBlobGet&InstranetImage=2734552&SecMode=1&DocId=2262340&Usage=2 [accessed: 05/23/2016].

Commissioner of Human Rights (2008): *Protecting the Right to Privacy in the Fight Against Terrorism*, available at: https://wcd.coe.int/com.instranet.InstraServlet?Index=no&command=com.instranet.CmdBlobGet&InstranetImage=1416463&SecMode=1&DocId=1426260&Usage=2 [accessed: 05/23/2016].

Connolly, Kate (2015): German secret service BND reduces cooperation with NSA, in: *The Guardian*, 05/07/2015, available at: http://www.theguardian.com/world/2015/may/07/german-secret-service-bnd-restricts-cooperation-nsa-us-online-surveillance-spy [accessed: 05/14/2016].

Conyers, John (2009): *Reining in the Imperial Presidency. Lessons and Recommendations Relating to the Presidency of George W. Bush. House Committee on the Judiciary Majority Staff Report to Chairman John C. Conyers, Jr.*, New York: Skyhorse Publishing.

Cope, Sophia (2016): House Advances Email Privacy Act, Setting the Stage for Vital Privacy Reform, 04/27/2016, available at: https://www.eff.org/deeplinks/2016/04/house-advances-email-privacy-act-setting-stage-vital-privacy-reform [accessed: 05/29/2016].

Council of Europe (2016 a): *Recommendation CM/Rec(2016)5[1] of the Committee of Ministers to member States on Internet freedom*, 04/13/2016, available at: https://search.coe.int/cm/Pages/result_details.aspx?ObjectId=09000016806415fa [accessed: 05/23/2016].

Council of Europe (2016 b): *Internet Governance – Council of Europe Strategy 2016–2019. Democracy, human rights and the rule of law in the digital world*, 03/30/2016, available at: https://search.coe.int/cm/Pages/result_details.aspx?ObjectId=09000016805c1b60 [accessed: 05/23/2016].

Council of Europe (2015 a): *Mass surveillance*, Resolution 2045, 04/21/2015, available at: http://assembly.coe.int/nw/xml/XRef/Xref-XML2HTML-en.asp?fileid=21692&lang=en [accessed: 05/23/2016].

Council of Europe (2015 b): *Improving the protection of whistleblowers*, Resolution 2060, 06/23/2015, available at: http://semantic-pace.net/tools/pdf.aspx?doc=aHRocDovL2Fzc2VtYmx5LmNvZS5pbnQvbncveG1sL1hSZWYvWDJILURXLWV4dHIuYXNwP2ZpbGVpZDoyMTkzMSZsYW5nPUVO&xsl=aHRocDovL3NlbWFudGljcGFjZS5uZXQvWHNsdC9QZGYvWFJlZi1XRC1BVC1YTUwyUERGLnhzbA==&xsltparams=ZmlsZWlkPTIxOTMx [accessed: 05/23/2015]

Council of Europe (2013 a): *Council of Europe alerts governments on risks of digital tracking and surveillance*, 06/12/2013, available at: https://go.coe.int/phA5g [accessed: 05/23/2016].

Council of Europe (2013 b): *Council of Europe ministerial conference calls for effective safeguards against electronic mass surveillance*, 11/08/2013, available at: https://go.coe.int/bjrvF [accessed: 05/23/2016].

Council of Europe (2001): *Additional Protocol to the Convention for the Protection of Individuals with regard to Automatic Processing of Personal Data regarding supervisory authorities and transborder data flows*, available at: http://www.coe.int/de/web/conventions/full-list/-/conventions/rms/0900001680080626 [accessed: 01/20/2016].

Council of Europe (1981): *Convention for the Protection of Individuals with regard to Automatic Processing of Personal Data*, available at: http://www.coe.int/de/web/conventions/full-list/-/conventions/rms/0900001680078b37 [accessed: 01/19/2016].

Council of Europe (n.d.a): *European Convention on Human Rights*, available at: http://www.echr.coe.int/Documents/Convention_ENG.pdf [accessed: 01/19/2016].

Council of Europe (n.d.b): *Ad Hoc Committee on Data Protection (CAHDATA)*, available at: http://www.coe.int/t/dghl/standardsetting/dataprotection/Cahdata_en.asp [accessed: 05/23/2016].

Council of Europe (n.d.c): *United States – Observer*, available at: http://www.coe.int/en/web/portal/united-states [accessed: 05/23/2016].

Cullather, Nick (2015): Security and Liberty: The Imaginary Balance, in: *The Snowden Reader*, David Fidler (ed.), Bloomington: Indiana University Press, pp. 19–25.

Daase, Christopher/Tim Nicholas Rühlig (2016): Der Wandel der Sicherheitskultur nach 9/11, in: *Innere Sicherheit nach 9/11. Sicherheitsbedrohungen und (immer) neue Sicherheitsmaßnahmen?*, Susanne Fischer/Carlo Masala (eds.), Wiesbaden: Springer VS Verlag, pp. 13–34.

Der Spiegel (1971): *EDV im Odenwald*, No. 20, p. 88, available at: http://www.spiegel.de/spiegel/print/d-43176393.html [accessed: 01/26/2016].

Deutscher Bundestag (2017): *Beschlussfassung und Bericht des 1. Untersuchungsausschusses nach Artikel 44 des Grundgesetzes*, Vorabfassung, 06/23/2017, Drucksache 18/12850, available at: http://dip21.bundestag.de/dip21/btd/18/128/1812850.pdf [accessed: 09/05/2017].

Diffie, Whitfield/Susan Landau (2007): *Privacy on the Line. The Politics of Wiretapping and Encryption*, Massachusetts: MIT Press.

Doherty, Thomas (2003): *Cold War, Cool Medium. Television, McCarthyism, and American Culture*, New York: Columbia University Press.

Dycus, Stephen (2008): Domestic military intelligence activities, in: *US National Security, Intelligence and Democracy. From the Church Committee to the War on Terror*, Russell Miller (ed.), Abingdon: Routledge, pp. 163–183.

Electronic Frontier Foundation (n.d.a): *About EFF*, available at: https://www.eff.org/about [accessed: 02/20/2015].

Electronic Frontier Foundation (n.d.b): *Timeline of NSA Domestic Spying*, available at: https://www.eff.org/nsa-spying/timeline [accessed: 05/04/2016].

Electronic Frontier Foundation (n.d.c): *All EFF's legal cases*, available at: https://www.eff.org/cases [accessed: 05/25/2016].

Electronic Privacy Information Center (n.d.): *About EPIC*, available at: https://epic.org/epic/about.html [accessed: 02/20/2015].

Elliff, John (1984): Attorney General's Guidelines for FBI Investigations, in: *Cornell Law Review*, Vol. 69, No. 4, pp. 785–815.

Elmer, Greg (2014): Panopticon – discipline – control, in: *Routledge Handbook of Surveillance Studies*, Kristie Ball et al. (eds.), Abingdon: Routledge, pp. 21–29.

Ennöckl, Daniel (2014): *Der Schutz der Privatsphäre in der elektronischen Datenverarbeitung*, Wien: Verlag Österreich.

European Data Protection Supervisor (2016): *EDPS starts work on a New Digital Ethics*, 01/26/2016, Press Release No. EPDS/2016/05, available at: https://secure.edps.europa.eu/EDPSWEB/webdav/site/mySite/shared/Documents/EDPS/PressNews/Press/2016/EDPS-2016-05-EDPS_Ethics_Advisory_Group_EN.pdf [accessed: 05/20/2016].

European Data Protection Supervisor (n.d.): *Ethics Advisory Group*, available at: https://secure.edps.europa.eu/EDPSWEB/edps/EDPS/Ethics [accessed: 05/20/2016].

European Parliament (2014): *European Parliament resolution of 12 March 2014 on the US NSA surveillance programme, surveillance bodies in various Member States and their impact on EU citizens' fundamental rights and on transatlantic cooperation in Justice and Home Affairs*, 03/12/2014, EU Doc. P7_TA(2014)0230, available at: http://www.europarl.europa.eu/sides/getDoc.do?pubRef=-//EP//NONSGML+TA+P7-TA-2014-0230+0+DOC+PDF+V0//EN [accessed: 05/19/2016].

European Parliament (2013): *European Parliament resolution of 4 July 2013 on the US National Security Agency surveillance programme, surveillance bodies in various Member States and their impact on EU citizens' privacy*, 07/04/2013, EU Doc. P7_TA(2013)0322, available at: http://www.europarl.europa.eu/sides/getDoc.do?pubRef=-//EP//NONSGML+TA+P7-TA-2013-0322+0+DOC+PDF+V0//EN [accessed: 05/19/2016].

European Parliament (2001): *Report on the existence of a global system for the interception of private and commercial communications (ECHELON interception system)*, 07/11/2001, EU Doc. A5-0264/2001, available at: http://www.europarl.europa.eu/sides/getDoc.do?pubRef=-//EP//TEXT+REPORT+A5-2001-0264+0+DOC+XML+V0//EN#_part5_def3 [accessed: 04/29/2016].

European Union (2016): Directive 2016/680 of the European Parliament and of the Council of 27 April 2016 on the protection of natural persons with regard to the processing of personal data by competent authorities for the purposes of the prevention, investigation, detection or prosecution of criminal offences or the execution of criminal penalties, and on the free movement of such data, and repealing Council Framework Decision 2008/977/JHA, in: *Official Journal of the European Union*, L 119, 05/04/2016, pp. 0089–0131, available at: http://eur-lex.europa.eu/legal-content/EN/TXT/PDF/?uri=CELEX:32016L0680&rid=2 [accessed: 05/19/2016].

European Union (2012): *Charter of Fundamental Rights of the European Union*, available at: http://eur-lex.europa.eu/legal-content/EN/TXT/?uri=CELEX:12012P/TXT [accessed: 01/21/2016].

European Union (1995): Directive 95/46/EC of the European Parliament and of the

Council of 24 October 1995 on the protection of individuals with regard to the processing of personal data and on the free movement of such data, in: *Official Journal of the European Union*, L 281, 11/23/1995, pp. 0031–0050, available at: http://eur-lex.europa.eu/LexUriServ/LexUriServ.do?uri=CELEX:31995L0046:en:HTML [accessed: 01/19/2016].

Fidler, David (ed.) (2015 a): *The Snowden Reader*, Bloomington: Indiana University Press.

Fidler, David (2015 b): U.S. Foreign Policy and the Snowden Leaks, in: *The Snowden Reader*, David Fidler (ed.), Bloomington: Indiana University Press, pp. 52–69.

Finnemore, Martha/Kathryn Sikkink (1998): International Norm Dynamics and Political Change, in: *International Organization*, Vol. 53, No. 4, pp. 887–917.

Foerstel, Herbert (2008): *The Patriot Act. A Documentary and Reference Guide*, Westport: Greenwood Press.

Forsythe, David (2002): The United States and International Criminal Justice, in: *Human Rights Quarterly*, Vol. 24, No. 4, pp. 974–991.

Gamson, William/David Meyer (1996): Framing Political Opportunity, in: *Comparative Perspectives on Social Movements: Political Opportunities, Mobilizing Structures, and Cultural Framings*, Dough McAdam et al. (eds.), Cambridge: Cambridge University Press, pp. 275–290.

Garstka, Hansjürgen (2003): Informationelle Selbstbestimmung und Datenschutz. Das Recht auf Privatsphäre, in: *Bürgerrechte im Netz*, Christiane Schulzki-Haddouti (ed.), pp. 48–70.

Gathmann, Florian (2013): Eklat um Evo Morales: Präsidentenjet verlässt Wien nach Zwölf-Stunden-Stopp, in: *Spiegel Online*, 07/03/2013, available at: http://www.spiegel.de/politik/ausland/morales-flugzeug-in-wien-gestoppt-snowden-nicht-an-bord-a-909146.html [accessed: 05/28/2016].

Gebauer, Matthias et al. (2013): Berlin Leaves Biggest NSA Questions Unanswered, in: *Spiegel Online*, 07/29/2013, available at: http://www.spiegel.de/international/world/german-government-responds-to-nsa-spying-and-data-collection-leaks-a-913635.html [accessed: 05/16/2016].

Gellman, Barton (2013): U.S. surveillance architecture includes collection of revealing Internet, phone metadata, in: *The Washington Post*, 06/16/2013, available at: https://www.washingtonpost.com/investigations/us-surveillance-architecture-includes-collection-of-revealing-internet-phone-metadata/2013/06/15/e9bf004a-d511-11e2-b05f-3ea3f0e7bb5a_print.html [accessed: 05/04/2016].

Gellman, Barton/Laura Poitras (2013): U.S., British intelligence mining data from nine U.S. Internet companies in broad secret program, in: *The Washington Post*, 06/07/2013, available at: https://www.washingtonpost.com/investigations/us-intelligence-mining-data-from-nine-us-internet-companies-in-broad-secret-program/2013/06/06/3a0c0da8-cebf-11e2-8845-d970ccb04497_story.html?hpid=z1 [accessed: 04/28/2016].

Gibbs, Samuel (2016): Data regulators reject EU-US Privacy Shield safe harbour deal, in: *The Guardian*, 04/14/2016, available at: https://www.theguardian.com/technology/2016/apr/14/data-regulators-reject-eu-us-privacy-shield-safe-harbour-deal [accessed: 05/19/2016].

Gibbs, Samuel (2015): What is 'safe harbour' and why did the EUCJ just declare it invalid?, in: *The Guardian*, 10/06/2015, available at: https://www.theguardian.com/technology/2015/oct/06/safe-harbour-european-court-declare-invalid-data-protection [accessed: 05/19/2016].

Gill, Peter (2015): World Society under Surveillance, in: *Global Trends: Prospects for World Society*, Stiftung Entwicklung und Frieden (ed.), pp. 71–86.

Gilliom, John/Torin Monahan (2014): Everyday resistance, in: *Routledge Handbook of Surveillance Studies*, Kristie Ball et. al. (ed.), Abingdon: Routledge, pp. 405–411.

Giugni, Marco (2009): Political Opportunities: From Tilly to Tilly, in: *Swiss Political Science Review*, Vol. 15, No. 2, pp. 361–368.

Glancy, Dorothy (1979): The Invention of the Right to Privacy, in: *Arizona Law Review*, Vol. 21, No. 1, pp. 1–39.

Glendon, Mary Ann (2002): *A World Made New. Eleanor Roosevelt and the Universal Declaration of Human Rights*, New York: Random House.

Global Privacy Enforcement Network (n.d.): *Action Plan for the Global Privacy Enforcement Network (GPEN)*, available at: https://www.privacyenforcement.net/about_the_network#action_plan [accessed: 01/20/2016].

Goos, Kerstin et al. (2015): The co-evolution of surveillance technologies and surveillance practices, in: *Surveillance in Europe*, David Wright/Reinhard Kreissl (ed.), New York: Routledge, pp. 51–100.

Gorman, Siobhan/Evan Perez/Janet Hook (2013): U.S. Collects Vast Data Trove, in: *The Wall Street Journal*, 06/07/2013, available at: http://www.wsj.com/article s/SB10001424127887324299104578529112289298922 [accessed: 04/27/2016].

Greenberg, Andy (2017): Passing the Email Privacy Act Has Never Been More Urgent, in: *Wired*, 02/06/2017, available at: https://www.wired.com/2017/02/trum p-power-email-privacy-act-never-urgent/ [accessed: 09/06/2017].

Greenberg, Andy (2014): These Are the Emails Snowden Sent to First Introduce His Epic NSA Leaks, in: *Wired*, 10/13/2014, available at: https://www.wired.co m/2014/10/snowdens-first-emails-to-poitras/ [accessed: 05/28/2016].

Greenberg, Andy (2013): Watch Top US Intelligence Officials Repeatedly Deny NSA Spying On Americans Over The Last Year, in: *Forbes*, 06/06/2013, available at: http://www.forbes.com/sites/andygreenberg/2013/06/06/watch-top-u-s-intelligence-officials-repeatedly-deny-nsa-spying-on-americans-over-the-last-y ear-videos/#6c8b4e1021d3 [accessed: 04/27/2016].

Greenberg, Ivan (2010): *The Dangers of Dissent. The FBI and Civil Liberties since 1965*, New York: Lexington.

Greenlee, Michael (2008): National security letters and intelligence oversight, in: *US National Security, Intelligence and Democracy. From the Church Committee to the War on Terror*, Russell Miller (ed.), Abingdon: Routledge, pp. 184–204.

Greenwald, Glenn (2013 a): NSA collecting phone records of millions of Verizon customers daily, in: *The Guardian*, 06/06/2013, available at: http://www.theguar dian.com/world/2013/jun/06/nsa-phone-records-verizon-court-order [accessed: 04/27/2016].

Greenwald, Glenn (2013 b): NSA collected US email records in bulk for more than two years under Obama, in: *The Guardian*, 06/27/2013, available at: http://www .theguardian.com/world/2013/jun/27/nsa-data-mining-authorised-obama [accessed: 04/28/2016].

Greenwald, Glenn/Spancer Ackerman (2013): Now the NSA is still harvesting your online data, in: *The Guardian*, 06/27/2013, available at: http://www.thegua rdian.com/world/2013/jun/27/nsa-online-metadata-collection [accessed: 05/04/2016].

Haas, Michael (2014): *International Human Rights. A Comprehensive Introduction*, New York: Routledge.

Hager, Nicky (2015): Wie die NSA in die Welt kam, in: *Die Überwacher. Prism, Google, Whistleblower*, Edition Le Monde diplomatique No. 16, Dorothee d ʼAprile (ed.), pp. 10–17.

Haggerty, Kevin/Richard Ericson (2000): The surveillant assemblage, in: *British Journal of Sociology*, Vol. 51, No. 4, pp. 605–622.

Harper, Nick (2014): FISA's Fuzzy Line between Domestic and International Terrorism, in: *The University of Chicago Law Review*, Vol. 81, No. 3, pp. 1123-1164.

Harris, Shane (2010): *The Watchers. The Rise of America´s Surveillance State*, New York: Penguin Press.

Hart, Gary (2008): Liberty and security, in: *US National Security, Intelligence and Democracy. From the Church Committee to the War on Terror*, Russell Miller (ed.), Abingdon: Routledge, pp. 13–21.

Hegemann, Hendrik/Martin Kahl (2016): Konstruktionen und Vorstellungen von Wirksamkeit in der Antiterror-Politik: Eine kritische Betrachtung, in: *Innere Sicherheit nach 9/11. Sicherheitsbedrohungen und (immer) neue Sicherheitsmaßnahmen?*, Susanne Fischer/Carlo Masala (eds.), Wiesbaden: Springer VS Verlag, pp. 189–207.

Heißler, Julian (2017): Ein bisschen Ausspähen unter Freunden, in: *tagesschau.de*, 10/21/2017, available at: https://www.tagesschau.de/inland/bnd-gesetz-reform-103.html [accessed: 09/05/2017].

Heller, Regina/Martin Kahl/Daniela Pisoiu (2012): The 'dark' side of normative argumentation – The case of counterterrorism policy, in: *Global Constitutionalism*, Vol. 1, No. 2, pp. 278–312.

Hempel, Leon/Susanne Krasmann/Ulrich Böckling (2011): Sichtbarkeitsregime: Eine Einleitung, in: *Sichtbarkeitsregime. Überwachung, Sicherheit und Privatheit im 21. Jahrhundert*, Leon Hempel et al. (eds.), Wiesbaden: VS Verlag für Sozialwissenschaften, pp. 7–24.

Holt, Jennifer/Steven Malcic (2015): The Privacy Ecosystem. Regulating Digital Identity in the United States and European Union, in: *Journal of Information Policy*, Vol. 5, pp. 155–178.

Horowitz, Sarah (2017): Foucault's Panopticon. A Model for NSA Surveillance?, in: *Privacy and Power. A Transatlantic Dialogue in the Shadow of the NSA-Affair*, Russel Miller (ed.), Cambridge: Cambridge University Press, pp. 39–62.

Jansen, Jonas (2015): So können Sie nachprüfen, ob Sie ausgespäht wurden, in: *Frankfurter Allgemeine Zeitung*, 02/19/2015, available at: http://www.faz.net/aktuell/feuilleton/debatten/privacy-international-zeigt-ueberwachung-durch-gchq-13437376.html [accessed: 02/20/2015].

Johnson, Brittany May (2016): Foreign National´s Privacy Interests Under U.S. Foreign Intelligence Law, in: *Texas International Law Journal*, Vol. 51, No. 2, pp. 229–257.

Johnson, Loch (2008): Establishment of modern intelligence accountability, in: *US National Security, Intelligence and Democracy. From the Church Committee to the War on Terror*, Russell Miller (ed.), Abingdon: Routledge, pp. 37–56.

Kammerer, Dietmar (2015): Absolut unamerikanisch. Die schleichende Enteignung der Privatsphäre in den USA, in: *Die Überwacher. Prism, Google, Whistleblower*, Edition Le Monde diplomatique No. 16, Dorothee d'Aprile (ed.), pp. 28–32.

Katzenstein, Peter (1996): *The Culture of National Security. Norms and Identity in World Politics*, New York: Columbia University Press.

Keck, Margaret/Kathryn Sikkink (1998): *Activists beyond Borders. Advocacy Networks in International Politics*, Ithaca: Cornell University Press.

Kerr, Orin (2001): The Fourth Amendment in Cyberspace: Can Encryption Create a "Reasonable Expectation to Privacy?", in: *Connecticut Law Review*, Vol. 33, No. 503, pp. 503–533.

Kietz, Daniela/Johannes Thimm (2013): Zwischen Überwachung und Aufklärung. Die amerikanische Debatte und die europäische Reaktion auf die Praxis der NSA, *SWP-Aktuell*, No. 51.

Kittlitz, Alard von (2010): Der Traum von einem idealen Leben, in: *Frankfurter Allgemeine Zeitung*, 08/06/2010, available at: http://www.faz.net/aktuell/feuilleton/debatten/digitales-denken/ende-der-privatsphaere-der-traum-von-einem-idealen-leben-11026194.html [accessed: 06/09/2016].

Krasmann, Susanne (2011): Der Präventionsstaat im Einvernehmen. Wie Sichtbarkeitsregime stillschweigend Akzeptanz produzieren, in: *Sichtbarkeitsregime. Überwachung, Sicherheit und Privatheit im 21. Jahrhundert*, Leon Hempel et al. (eds.), Wiesbaden: VS Verlag für Sozialwissenschaften, pp. 53–70.

Krieger, Wolfgang (2014): *Geschichte der Geheimdienste. Von den Pharaonen bis zur NSA*, München: C.H. Beck.

Kurz, Constanze (2016): Wir erklären den Cyber War für eröffnet, in: *Frankfurter Allgemeine Zeitung*, 03/07/16, available at: http://www.faz.net/aktuell/feuilleton/aus-dem-maschinenraum/amerika-erklaert-dem-is-den-ersten-cyberwar-14109024.html [accessed: 04/18/16].

Lee, Newton (2015): *Counterterrorism and Cybersecurity. Total Information Awareness*, Heidelberg: Springer.

Liese, Andrea (2009): Exceptional Necessity. How Liberal Democracies Contest the Prohibition of Torture and Ill-Treatment when Countering Terrorism, in: *Journal of International Law and International Relations*, Vol. 5, No. 1, pp. 17–47.

Liptak, Adam (2013): Justices Turn Back Challenge to Broader US Eavesdropping, in: *The New York Times*, 02/26/2013, available at: http://www.nytimes.com/2013/02/27/us/politics/supreme-court-rejects-challenge-to-fisa-surveillance-law.html?_r=0 [accessed: 05/24/2016].

Lynch, Andrew/Nicola McGarrity/George Williams (2010): The emergence of a 'culture of control,' in: *Counter-Terrorism and Beyond. The Culture of Law and Justice after 9/11*, Nicola McGarrity et al. (eds.), London: Routledge, pp. 3–9.

Lyon, David (2015): *Surveillance after Snowden*, Cambridge: Polity. Lyon, David/Kevin Haggerty/Kristie Ball (2014): Introducing surveillance studies,

in: *Routledge Handbook of Surveillance Studies*, Kristie Ball et al. (eds.), Abingdon: Routledge, pp. 1–11.

MacAskill, Ewen (2015): The NSA's bulk metadata collection authority just expired. What now?, in: *The Guardian*, 11/28/2015, available at: http://www.theguardian.com/us-news/2015/nov/28/nsa-bulk-metadata-collection-expires-usa-freedom-act [accessed: 05/29/2016].

Mason, Alpheus Thomas (1946): *Brandeis. A free man's life*, New York: Viking Press.

McCullagh, Declan (2006): FBI taps cell phone mic as eavesdropping tool, available at: http://www.cnet.com/news/fbi-taps-cell-phone-mic-as-eavesdropping-tool/ [accessed: 04/16/16].

McCulloch, Jude/Sharon Pickering (2010): Counter-terrorism. The law and policing of pre-emption, in: in: *Counter-Terrorism and Beyond. The Culture of Law and Justice after 9/11*, Nicola McGarrity et al. (eds.), London: Routledge, pp. 13–29.

McGarrity, Nicola/George Williams (2010): When extraordinary measures become normal. Pre-emption in counter-terrorism and other laws, in: *Counter-Terrorism and Beyond. The Culture of Law and Justice after 9/11*, Nicola McGarrity et al. (eds.), London: Routledge, pp. 131–149.

McKeown, Ryder (2009): Norm Regress: US Revisionism and the Slow Death of the Torture Norm, in: *International Relations*, Vol. 23, No. 1, pp. 5–25.

Meister, Andre (2013): Vorratsdatenspeicherung: Warum Verbindungsdaten noch aussagekräftiger sind als Kommunikationsinhalte, in: *Überwachtes Netz. Edward Snowden und der größte Überwachungsskandal der Geschichte*, Markus Beckendahl/Andre Meister (eds.), Berlin: newthinking communications, pp. 229–233.

Miller, Russel (2017): A Rose by any Other Name? The Comparative Law of the NSA-Affair, in: *Privacy and Power. A Transatlantic Dialogue in the Shadow of the NSA-Affair*, Russel Miller (ed.), Cambridge: Cambridge University Press, pp. 63–94.

Mills, Jon L. (2015): The Future of Privacy in the Surveillance Age, in: *After Snowden. Privacy, Secrecy, and Security in the Information Age*, Ronald Goldfarb (ed.), New York: St. Martin's Press, pp. 191–260.

Moechel, Erich (2013): Was Metadaten der NSA verraten, in: *Überwachtes Netz. Edward Snowden und der größte Überwachungsskandal der Geschichte*, Markus Beckendahl/Andre Meister (eds.), Berlin: newthinking communications, pp. 241–244.

Montgomery, Bruce (2008): *The Bush-Cheney Administration's Assault on Open Government*, Westport: Praeger.

Muižnieks, Nils (2015): Europe is spying on you, in: *The New York Times*, 10/27/2015, available at: http://www.nytimes.com/2015/10/28/opinion/europe-is-spying-on-you-mass-surveillance.html?_r=0 [accessed: 05/23/2015].

Mužnieks, Nils (2013): Prism: secret surveillance could destroy democracy rather than defend it, in: *The Guardian*, 06/26/2013, available at: http://www.coe.int/en/web/commissioner/-/prism-secret-surveillance-could-destroy-democracy-rather-than-defend-it [accessed: 05/23/2016].

Nakashima, Ellen/Jobby Warrick (2013): For NSA chief, terrorist threat drives passion to 'collect it all', in: *The Washington Post*, 07/14/2013, available at: https://www.washingtonpost.com/world/national-security/for-nsa-chief-terrorist-threat-drives-passion-to-collect-it-all/2013/07/14/3d26ef80-ea49-11e2-a301-ea5a8116d211_story.html [accessed: 06/08/2016].

Newell, Jim (2013): Thousands gather in Washington for anti-NSA 'Stop Watching Us' rally, in: *The Guardian*, 10/26/2013, available at: http://www.theguardian.com/world/2013/oct/26/nsa-rally-stop-watching-washington-snowden [accessed: 06/08/2016].

Nielsen, Richard/Beth Simmons (2015): Rewards for Ratification: Payoffs for Participating in the International Human Rights Regime?, in: *International Studies Quarterly*, Vol. 59, No. 2, pp. 197–208.

Nissenbaum, Helen (2010): *Privacy in Context. Technology, Policy, and the Integrity of Social Life*, Stanford: Stanford University Press.

Nyst, Carly/Tomaso Falchetta (2017): The Right to Privacy in the Digital Age, in: *Journal of Human Rights Practice*, Vol. 9, No. 1, pp. 104–118.

Obama, Barack (2014): Remarks on Review of Signals Intelligence, in: *The Snowden Reader*, David Fidler (ed.), Bloomington: Indiana University Press, pp. 318–330.

O'Connel, Mary Ellen (2012): Cyber Security without Cyber War, in: *Journal of Conflict and Security Law*, Vol. 17, No. 2, pp. 187–209.

On the Issue (n.d.): *George W. Bush on Technology*, available at: http://www.ontheissues.org/Celeb/George_W__Bush_Infrastructure.htm [accessed: 05/03/2016].

Opitz, Sven/Ute Tellmann (2011): Katastrophale Szenarien: Gegenwärtige Zukunft in Ökonomie und Recht, in: *Sichtbarkeitsregime. Überwachung, Sicherheit und Privatheit im 21. Jahrhundert*, Leon Hempel et al. (eds.), Wiesbaden: VS Verlag für Sozialwissenschaften, pp. 27–52.

Organization for Economic Co-Operation and Development (2013): *The OECD Privacy Framework*, available at: http://www.oecd.org/sti/ieconomy/oecd_privacy_framework.pdf [accessed: 01/20/2016].

Organization for Economic Co-Operation and Development (1997): *Recommendation of the Council concerning guidelines for cryptography policy*, available at: http://www.oecd.org/officialdocuments/publicdisplaydocumentpdf/?cote=C(97)62/FINAL&docLanguage=En [accessed: 01/20/2016].

Organization for Economic Co-Operation and Development (1980): *OECD Guidelines on the Protection of Privacy and Transborder Flows of Personal Data*, available at: http://www.oecd.org/sti/ieconomy/oecdguidelinesontheprotectionofprivacyandtransborderflowsofpersonaldata.htm [accessed: 01/18/2016].

Panke, Diana/Ulrich Petersohn (2016): Norm challenges and norm death: The inexplicable?, in: *Cooperation and Conflict*, Vol. 51, No. 1, pp. 3–19.

Peters, Anne (2017): Privacy, *Rechtsstaatlichkeit*, and the Legal Limits on Extraterritorial Surveillance, in: *Privacy and Power. A Transatlantic Dialogue in the Shadow of the NSA-Affair*, Russel Miller (ed.), Cambridge: Cambridge University Press, pp. 145–179.

Pöschl, Magdalena (2015): Sicherung grund- und menschenrechtlicher Standards gegenüber neuen Gefährdungen durch private und ausländische Akteure, in: *Öffnung der öffentlich-rechtlichen Methode durch Internationalität und Interdisziplinarität: Erscheinungsformen, Chancen, Grenzen ; Referate und Diskussionen auf der Tagung der Vereinigung der Deutschen Staatsrechtslehrer in Düsseldorf vom 1. bis 4. Oktober 2014*, Hans Christian Röhl et al. (eds.), Berlin: de Gruyter, pp. 405–452.

Prosser, William (1960): Privacy, in: *California Law Review*, Vol. 48, No. 3, pp. 383–423.

Reagan, Priscilla M. (2014): Regulating surveillance technologies. Institutional arrangements, in: *Routledge Handbook of Surveillance Studies*, Kristie Ball et. al. (ed.), Abingdon: Routledge, pp. 397-404.

Rebinger, Simon (2017): *Datenschützer rätseln: Schafft Trump Datenschutz-Abkommen zwischen USA und EU ab?*, 01/27/2017, available at: https://netzpolitik.org/2017/datenschuetzer-raetseln-schafft-trump-datenschutz-abkommen-zwischen-usa-und-eu-ab/ [accessed: 09/07/2017].

Reilly, Mollie (2013): Obama Defends NSA Surveillance Program, Says It's 'Transparent,' in: *The Huffington Post*, 06/18/2013, available at: http://www.huffingtonpost.com/2013/06/17/obama-nsa-surveillance_n_3455771.html [accessed: 05/28/2016].

Restore the Fourth (2015): *Who we are*, 12/05/2015, available at: https://restorethe4th.com/who-we-are/ [accessed: 06/08/2016].

Risen, James (2013): Snowden Says He Took No Secret Files to Russia, in: *The New York Times*, 10/17/2013, available at: http://www.nytimes.com/2013/10/18/world/snowden-says-he-took-no-secret-files-to-russia.html?_r=0&mtrref=undefined&gwh=8BB37884F4339E8D704EFD583EF66B2E&gwt=pay [accessed: 05/28/2016].

Risen, James/Eric Lichtblau (2005): Bush Lets US Spy on Callers Without Courts, in: *The New York Times*, 12/16/2005, available at: http://www.nytimes.com/2005/12/16/politics/bush-lets-us-spy-on-callers-without-courts.html [accessed: 05/04/2016].

Risse, Thomas et al. (eds.) (2013): *The Persistent Power of Human Rights. From Commitment to Compliance*, New York: Cambridge University Press.

Risse, Thomas et al. (eds.) (1999): *The Power of Human Rights. International Norms and Domestic Change*, New York: Cambridge University Press.

Rössler, Beate (2001): *Der Wert des Privaten*, Frankfurt a.M.: Suhrkamp.

Roth, Anna-Lena/Florian Gathmann (2013): Merkel zur Handy-Affäre: "Ausspähen unter Freunden – das geht gar nicht", in: *Spiegel Online*, 10/24/2013, available at: http://www.spiegel.de/politik/deutschland/handy-spaehaffaere-um-merkel-regierung-ueberprueft-alle-nsa-erklaerungen-a-929843.html [accessed: 05/20/2016].

Rouseff, Dilma (2013): Statement to United Nations General Assembly, in: *The Snowden Reader*, David Fidler (ed.), Bloomington: Indiana University Press, pp. 158–159.

Rudl, Thomas (2016): *EU-US-Datenschutzschild: Irische Datenschützer reichen Nichtigkeitsklage ein*, 10/27/2016, available at: https://netzpolitik.org/2016/eu-us-datenschutzschild-irische-datenschuetzer-reichen-nichtigkeitsklage-ein/ [accessed: 09/07/2017].

Rudl, Thomas (2015): *Snowden-Dokumente bestätigen Echelon-Programm: Rückschau auf 40 Jahre Aufdeckungsarbeit*, 08/06/2015, available at: https://netzpolitik.org/2015/snowden-dokumente-bestaetigen-echelon-programm-rueckschau-auf-40-jahre-aufdeckungsarbeit/ [accessed: 04/29/2016].

Ruhmann, Ingo (2014): NSA, IT-Sicherheit und die Folgen, in: *Datenschutz und Datensicherheit*, No. 1/2014, pp. 40–46.

Rule, James (2014): "Needs" for surveillance and the movement to privacy, in: *Routledge Handbook of Surveillance Studies*, Kristie Ball et al. (eds.), Abingdon: Routledge, pp. 64–71.

Sales, Allice (2015): Brazil Shows How Not to Respond to Snowden Revelations, in: *Panam Post*, 02/24/2015, available at: https://panampost.com/alice-salles/2015/02/24/brazil-shows-how-not-to-respond-to-snowden-revelations/ [accessed: 05/15/2016].

Schaar, Peter (2013): Welche Konsequenzen haben PRISM und Tempora für den Datenschutz in Deutschland und Europa?, in: *Überwachtes Netz. Edward Snowden und der größte Überwachungsskandal der Geschichte*, Markus Beckendahl/Andre Meister (eds.), Berlin: newthinking communications, pp. 118–127.

Schariatmadari, David (2015): Privacy is starting to seem like a very 20th-century anomaly, in: *The Guardian*, 11/07/2015, available at: http://www.theguardian.com/commentisfree/2015/nov/07/privacy-seems-20th-century-aberration-but-worth-mourning [accessed: 01/26/2016].

Scheer, Ursula (2015): Haben die Amerikaner den Deutschen gedroht?, in: *Frankfurter Allgemeine Zeitung*, 03/20/2015, available at: http://www.faz.net/aktuell/feuilleton/medien/geheimdienste-und-snowden-gabriel-verraet-greenwald-ein-geheimnis-13496416.html [accessed: 05/28/2016].

Schiedermair, Stephanie (2012): *Der Schutz des Privaten als internationales Grundrecht*, Tübingen: Mohr Siebeck.

Schmale, Wolfgang/Marie-Theres Tinnefeld (2014): *Privatheit im digitalen Zeitalter*, Wien: Böhlau.

Schneider, Jens-Peter (2017): Developments in European Data Protection Law in the Shadow of the NSA-Affair, in: *Privacy and Power. A Transatlantic Dialogue in the Shadow of the NSA-Affair*, Russel Miller (ed.), Cambridge: Cambridge University Press, pp. 539–563.

Schrecker, Ellen (2002): *The Age of McCarthyism. A Brief History with Documents*, New York: Bedford/St. Martin's.

Schrecker, Ellen (1998): *Many are the Crimes. McCarthyism in America*, Princeton: Princeton University Press.

Schwartz, Paul (2013): The EU-U.S. Privacy Collision: A Turn to Institutions and Procedures, in: *Harvard Law Review*, Vol. 126, pp. 1967–2009.

Schwarz, Frederick (2008): The Church Committee, then and now, in: *US National Security, Intelligence and Democracy. From the Church Committee to the War on Terror*, Russell Miller (ed.), Abingdon: Routledge, pp. 22–36.

Schweidler, Walter (2014): *Der gute Staat. Politische Ethik von Platon bis zur Gegenwart*, Wiesbaden: Springer VS.

Scott, Mark (2016): U.S. and Europe in 'Safe Harbor' Data Deal, but Legal Fight May Await, in: *The New York Times*, 02/02/2016, available at: http://www.nytimes.com/2016/02/03/technology/us-europe-safe-harbor-data-deal.html?_r=0 [accessed: 05/19/2016].

Shance, Scott (2013): No Morsel Too Minuscule for All-Consuming N.S.A., in: *The New York Times*, 11/02/2013, available at: http://www.nytimes.com/2013/11/03/world/no-morsel-too-minuscule-for-all-consuming-nsa.html?pagewanted=1&_r=1 [accessed: 05/20/2016].

Shapiro, Ari (2013): How Obama's Response To NSA Spying Has Evolved, in: *NPR*, 11/13/2013, available at: http://www.npr.org/sections/itsallpolitics/2013/11/13/245037300/how-obamas-response-to-nsa-spying-has-evolved [accessed: 05/28/2016].

Sikkink, Kathryn (2013): The United States and torture: does the spiral model work?, in: *The Persistent Power of Human Rights. From Commitment to Compliance*, Thomas Risse et al. (eds.), New York: Cambridge University Press, pp. 145–163.

Smale, Alison (2015): Germany, Too, Is Accused of Spying on Friends, in: *The New York Times*, 05/05/2015, available at: http://www.nytimes.com/2015/05/06/world/europe/scandal-over-spying-shakes-german-government.html?_r=0 [accessed: 05/16/2016].

Solove, Daniel/Paul Schwartz (2009): *Privacy, Information and Technology*, New York: Wolters Kluwer.

Solove, Daniel (2008): *Understanding privacy*, Cambridge: Harvard University Press.

Solove, Daniel (2002): Conceptualizing Privacy, in: *California Law Review*, Vol. 90, No.4, pp. 1087–1155.

Sprenger, Florian (2015): *Politik der Mikroentscheidungen: Edward Snowden, Netzneutralität und die Architektur des Internets*, Lüneburg: meson press.

Stratford, Jean Slemmons/Juri Stratford (1998): Data Protection and Privacy in the United States and Europe, in: *IASSIST Quarterly*, Fall edition, pp. 17–20.

Theoharis, Athan (2011): *Abuse of Power. How Cold War Surveillance and Secrecy Policy Shaped the Response to 9/11*, Philadelphia: Temple University Press.

The White House (2014): *Presidential Policy Directive – Signals Intelligence Activities. Presidential Policy Directive/PPD-28*, available at: https://www.whitehouse.gov/the-press-office/2014/01/17/presidential-policy-directive-signals-intelligence-activities [accessed: 06/09/2016].

The White House (2002): *President Bush Delivers Graduation Speech at West Point*, available at: http://georgewbush-whitehouse.archives.gov/news/releases/2002/06/20020601-3.html [accessed: 04/28/2016].

Tilly, Charles (1978): *From Mobilization to Revolution*, Reading: Addison-Wesley Publishing.

United Nations (n.d.): *Charter of the United Nations*, available at: http://www.un.org/en/sections/un-charter/chapter-i/index.html [accessed: 06/12/2016].

United Nations General Assembly (2016): *Report of the Special Rapporteur on the right to privacy*, UN Doc. A/71/368, distributed on 08/30/2016, available at: http://www.un.org/en/ga/search/view_doc.asp?symbol=A/71/368 [accessed: 09/05/2017].

United Nations General Assembly (2014): *Promotion and protection of human rights and fundamental freedoms while countering terrorism. Report of the Special Rapporteur on the promotion and protection of human rights and fundamental freedoms while countering terrorism*, UN Doc. A/69/397, distributed on 09/23/2014, available at: http://www.un.org/en/ga/search/view_doc.asp?symbol=A/69/397 [accessed: 05/17/2016].

United Nations General Assembly (2013): *Resolution 68/167, The Right to Privacy in the Digital Age*, 13/18/2013, UN Doc. A/RES/68/167, distributed on 01/21/2014, available at: http://www.un.org/ga/search/view_doc.asp?symbol=A/RES/68/167 [accessed: 05/17/2016].

United Nations General Assembly (1998): *Official Records, Fifty-third session, 7th plenary meeting*, 11/211998, UN Doc. A/53/PV.7, available at: http://www.un.org/documents/a53pv 7.pdf [accessed: 06/13/2016].

United Nations General Assembly (1968): *Resolution 2450 (XXIII). Human rights and scientific and technological developments*, available at: https://documents-dds-ny.un.org/doc/RESOLUTION/GEN/NR0/244/10/IMG/NR024410.pdf?OpenElement [accessed: 01/17/2016].

United Nations Human Rights Council (2016): *Report of the Special Rapporteur on the right to privacy, Joseph A. Cannataci*, Advanced Unedited Version, UN Doc. A/HRC/31/64, distributed on 03/08/2016, available at: http://www.ohchr.org/EN/Issues/Privacy/SR/Pages/SRPrivacyIndex.aspx [accessed: 05/17/2016].

United Nations Human Rights Council (2014 a): *The right to privacy in the digital age. Report of the Office of the United Nations High Commissioner for Human Rights*, UN Doc. A/HRC/27/37, distributed on 06/30/2014, available at: http://www.ohchr.org/EN/Issues/DigitalAge/Pages/DigitalAgeIndex.aspx [accessed: 05/17/2016].

United Nations Human Rights Council (2014 b): *Concluding observations on the fourth periodic report of the United States of America*, 04/23/2014, UN Doc. CCPR/C/USA/CO/4, available at: http://www.refworld.org/docid/5374afcd4.html [accessed: 05/18/2016].

United States Government Publishing Office (2001): *Uniting and strengthening America by Providing Appropriate Tools Required to Intercept and Obstruct Terrorism (USA PATRIOT ACT) Act of 2001*, available at: https://www.gpo.gov/fdsys/pkg/PLAW-107publ56/pdf/PLAW-107publ56.pdf [accessed: 04/19/16].

Van Schaack, Beth (2014): The United States' Position on the Extraterritorial Application of Human Rights Obligations: Now is the Time for Change, in: *International Law Studies*, Vol. 90, pp. 20–65.

Vöeneky, Silja (2017): Espionage, Security Interests, and Human Rights in the Second Machine Age. NSA Mass Surveillance and the Framework of Public International Law, in: *Privacy and Power. A Transatlantic Dialogue in the Shadow of the NSA-Affair*, Russel Miller (ed.), Cambridge: Cambridge University Press, pp. 492–507.

Walen, Alec (2017): Forth Amendment Rights for Nonresident Aliens, in: *Privacy and Power. A Transatlantic Dialogue in the Shadow of the NSA-Affair*, Russel Miller (ed.), Cambridge: Cambridge University Press, pp. 282–303.

Warren, Samuel/Louis Brandeis (1890): The Right to Privacy, in: *Harvard Law Review*, Vol. 4, No. 5, pp. 193–220.

Weadon, Patrick D. (2009): *Sigsaly Story*, available at: https://www.nsa.gov/about/cryptologic_heritage/center_crypt_history/publications/sigsaly_story.shtml [Accessed: 01/14/2016].

Weisselberg, Charles (2010): Constitutional criminal procedure and civil rights in the shadow of the 'war on terror.' A look at recent United States decisions and the rhetoric of terrorism, in: *Counter-Terrorism and Beyond. The Culture of Law and Justice after 9/11*, Nicola McGarrity et al. (eds.), London: Routledge, pp. 71–87.

Westin, Alan (1970): *Privacy and Freedom*, New York: Ahteneum.

Wiener, Antje (2014): *A Theory of Contestation*, Heidelberg: Springer.

Winterfeld, Steve/Jason Andress (2013): *The Basics of Cyber Warfare. Understanding the Fundamentals of Cyber Warfare in Theory and Practice*, New York: Elsevier.

Wheeler, Brian (2004): 'This goes no further…', in: *BBC news*, 03/02/04, available at: http://news.bbc.co.uk/2/hi/uk_news/magazine/3522137.stm [accessed: 04/19/16].

Wright, David/Reinhard Kreissl (2015): European responses to the Snowden revelations, in: *Surveillance in Europe*, David Wright/Reinhard Kreissl (eds.), London: Routledge, pp. 6–50.

Zedner, Lucia (2009): *Security*, New York: Routledge.

Zengerle, Patricia (2013): U.S. lawmakers want sanctions on any country taking in Snowden, in: *Reuters*, 07/25/2013, available at: http://www.reuters.com/article/us-usa-security-congress-idUSBRE96O18220130725 [accessed: 05/28/2016].

Zurawski, Nils (2015): *Technische Innovationen und deren gesellschaftliche Auswirkungen im Kontext von Überwachung*, Schriftenreihe Sicherheit, Nr. 16, Jochen Schiller et al. (eds.), Berlin: Forschungsforum Öffentliche Sicherheit.

Zeitfracht Medien GmbH
Ferdinand-Jühlke-Straße 7
99095 Erfurt, Deutschland
produktsicherheit@kolibri360.de